General editors
William C. Carroll: Boston University
Brian Gibbons: University of Münster
Tiffany Stern: University College, Oxford

CONTRAST → knowing characters &
naïve characters.

...y manipulated, *and incidents are*
crosswated

Reconstruction of an Elizabethan Theatre
by C. Walter Hodges

...body Eget & Horner embissary

NEW MERMAIDS

NEW MERMAIDS

WILLIAM WYCHERLEY

THE COUNTRY WIFE

edited by James Ogden

Formerly University College of Wales,
Aberystwyth

Methuen Drama • London

New Mermaids

5 7 9 10 8 6 4

Second edition 1991

Methuen Drama
A & C Black Publishers Limited
36 Soho Square, London W1D 3QY
www.methuendrama.com

© 1991 A&C Black Publishers Limited

First New Mermaid edition 1973
© 1973 Ernest Benn Limited

A CIP catalogue record for this book is
available from the British Library

ISBN: 978 0 7136 6688 5

Printed in the UK by CPI Cox & Wyman, Reading, RG1 8EX

CONTENTS

ACKNOWLEDGEMENTS

Most of the work on this edition was done in Aberystwyth. I am grateful to the University College of Wales for granting me a term's study leave, and to members of the English Department, the Hugh Owen Library, and the National Library of Wales especially my colleagues Peter Bement, Mike Smith, Richard Brinkley and Ron Job, for help in various ways. I also spent some time in Cambridge University Library, where I was assisted by Elizabeth Erskine and Brian Jenkins. I am deeply indebted to previous editors, especially John Dixon Hunt, the late Thomas Fujimura, Gerald Weales, David Cook and John Swannell, Arthur Friedman, Peter Holland, and Peter Dixon. Some acknowledgement of these debts is made in the notes. Correspondents who gave useful advice and encouragement were Arthur Scouten, Edward Langhans, Stuart Sillars, Frank Lamport, and of course the general editor of the New Mermaids, Brian Gibbons. For the publishers, Anne Watts and Margaret Parker helped me to deal with problems of presentation. Mrs Jean Cock did an excellent job on the typescript. Tom Craik and Richard Brinkley helped generously with the 1997 revisions.

JAMES OGDEN

INTRODUCTION

THE AUTHOR

WYCHERLEY WOULD KNOW that the true poet 'ought himself to be a true poem', as Milton put it,[1] but his life compared with his plays seems shapeless; certainly we lack information to see a pattern, but perhaps he lacked power to create one.

At the time of Wycherley's birth, his family had been living in Shropshire for two centuries or more, and their estate at Clive was worth about £600 a year.[2] His father, Daniel Wycherley, had become steward to the Marquess of Winchester; his mother, Bethia Shrimpton, had been an attendant to the Marchioness. William was probably born on 28 March 1641, and he was baptised at Whitchurch, Hampshire, on 8 April that year. Daniel Wycherley was an able man, who inherited the family estate and increased its value, but became so engrossed in lawsuits as to prefigure Dickens's 'Man from Shropshire' in *Bleak House*. Bethia Shrimpton, 'who if she wanted beauty had a large share of tongue', was another strong character, though much of her time would be spent in domesticity and childbearing; there were three sons and two daughters after William.[3]

Daniel looked after his eldest son's education, and in 1656 William was sent to France to join the *précieux* salon of Madame de Montausier at Angoulême. Here he was converted to Roman Catholicism, and would meet many who were prominent in French life, including the Marquis de Montausier, who has been seen as the original of Alceste in Molière's *Le Misanthrope*, and so perhaps of Manly in Wycherley's *The Plain Dealer*. Shortly before the Restoration he returned to England; he was admitted to the Inner Temple, London, in 1659, and went to Queen's College, Oxford, in 1660. At Oxford he probably reverted to Protestantism, but he did not matriculate. He was soon back in London leading the life of a fashionable gentleman and aspiring courtier, which included occasional military service. He was in Ireland with the Earl of Arran's regiment in 1662, he

---

[1] *An Apology against a Pamphlet* (1641). Ben Jonson had remarked on 'the impossibility of any man's being the good poet, without first being a good man' in the prefatory epistle to *Volpone* (1607).

[2] Richardson Pack, 'Memoirs of Mr. Wycherley's Life', in Wycherley's *Posthumous Works*, ed. Lewis Theobald (1728), p. 5. G.E. Aylmer, *The King's Servants* (Routledge, 1974), p. 331, estimates average annual income for 1633: peers, £6000; knights, £800; esquires, £500; gentlemen, £150.

[3] The standard biography is B. Eugene McCarthy's *William Wycherley* (Ohio University Press, 1979), but for Wycherley's birth see Friedman, pp. xiii–xiv footnote, and for his mother see Richard Gough, *The History of Myddle*, ed. David Hey (Penguin, 1981), p. 140.

probably served at sea in the Second Dutch War in 1665, and he was made a Captain in the Duke of Buckingham's regiment in 1672.

Meanwhile Wycherley's literary career began with occasional poems and the anonymous publication of *Hero and Leander in Burlesque* in 1669. His first two plays, *Love in a Wood* and *The Gentleman Dancing-Master*, were performed in 1671 and 1672, the former by the King's Company at the Bridges Street theatre, the latter by the Duke's at Dorset Garden. There is a story that the success of *Love in a Wood* and the handsome appearance of its author excited Charles II's ex-mistress Barbara Villiers, Lady Castlemaine, and that Wycherley became one of her lovers. Certainly the King himself 'was extremely fond of him upon account of his wit',[4] and he became friendly with Buckingham and other courtiers. With the performances by the King's Company at Drury Lane of *The Country Wife* in 1675 and *The Plain Dealer* in 1676 he established himself as the leading writer of satirical comedy. The success of the latter owed something to the 'loud approbation' of his aristocratic friends, and led to his becoming known after its principal character as 'the Plain Dealer' or 'Manly'. Dryden summarised these impressions when he referred to 'the satire, wit, and strength of manly Wycherley'.[5]

As Wycherley lived almost another forty years, but did not write another play, the rest of his life makes depressing reading. He suffered various misfortunes, and made numerous mistakes. In 1677 he was seriously ill with a fever which undermined his health and affected his memory. King Charles visited him at his lodgings, paid for a convalescence abroad, and later made him tutor to his bastard son the Duke of Richmond at a salary of £1500 a year. But meanwhile the temperamental Countess of Drogheda had fallen for Wycherley, and on the death of her husband in June 1679 they secretly married; when Charles got to hear about it, Wycherley lost favour.

Wycherley's wife was a financial liability, as she had personal debts, and her late husband's will was contested by the family. When she died in 1685 her will was contested by the family too, and Wycherley was involved in seemingly endless lawsuits, just like his father. Soon he was committed to the Fleet Prison for debts amounting to over £1500. He asked his friend the Earl of Mulgrave for help, and Mulgrave apparently arranged a court performance of *The Plain Dealer* before the new king, James II. James liked the play, and perhaps the playwright pleased him further by professing his Roman Catholicism; anyway Wycherley was released, presented with £500, and granted an annual pension of £200; and these kindnesses 'made

---

[4] Pack (note 2), p. 8
[5] 'To my Dear Friend Mr. Congreve' (1694)

Mr Wycherley always a Jacobite'.[6] But of course when James lost his throne, Wycherley lost his pension. His financial problems and associated lawsuits continued at least until the death of his father and his inheritance of Clive Hall in 1697.

Wycherley's literary achievements, civilised manners, and witty conversation enabled him to retain the respect of the younger men of letters who gathered at Will's Coffee House near his London lodgings. He announced the publication of his miscellaneous *Poems*, but it was some eight years before they appeared in 1704, and the poems themselves were unworthy of him, as he partly knew. At about this time Alexander Pope sought his friendship to enter the literary world, and Wycherley got Pope's help to revise the poems.

Pope says Wycherley told him he would not marry again till he was on his deathbed, and Wycherley was certainly dying when he married Elizabeth Jackson on 20 December 1715. She was supposed to be an heiress, but was in fact the mistress of his unscrupulous cousin Thomas Shrimpton. At the time of the marriage Wycherley also received Extreme Unction according to the Roman Catholic rite; Pope joked about the sequence of sacraments and recorded Wycherley's humorous advice to his wife, 'Never marry an old man again'.[7] Wycherley died on New Year's Eve and was buried at St Paul's, Covent Garden; Shrimpton married his widow, and after more litigation took control of his estate. It is a sad irony that the dramatist's life should have ended with such farcical scenes.

The Play

Our scene is London; the time, 1675. The characters appear in the elaborate costume of Restoration ladies and gentlemen before familiar scenes of fashionable lodgings, houses, and places of resort. They speak mainly in prose; which, as we may know, Molière's *bourgeois gentilhomme* found to his surprise he had been doing all his life.[8] That is to say, while their speech is stylised and theatrical – allowing them memorable witticisms, pointed asides, good exit lines, and couplets at the ends of the Acts – it is only what we Restoration ladies and gentlemen ourselves aspire to; Sparkish even claims that some of us 'speak more wit' than the silly rogues who write our plays (III. ii. 98–100). But as life does not throw up eccentric characters and

[6] Charles Gildon, *Memoirs of the Life of William Wycherley* (1718), pp. 7–8

[7] Letter from Pope to Edward Blount, 21 January 1715/16, in *The Correspondence of Alexander Pope*, ed. George Sherburn (Oxford, 1956), vol. 1, pp. 328–9. See also H.P. Vincent, 'The Death of William Wycherley', *Harvard Studies and Notes*, vol. 15 (1933), 219–42.

[8] Molière, *Le Bourgeois Gentilhomme* II.iv, in *Oeuvres Complètes*, ed. Georges Couton (Gallimard, 1971), vol. 2, p. 730

farcical situations with such regularity, we scarcely suppose we are being given a realistic view of it, and we may be transported into a purely theatrical world. For audiences today, this effect may be reinforced by the costumes and scenery of a remote and incredible period; yet the temptation to escape into fantasy should be resisted. If we can see the characters and situations as exaggerating those of ordinary life for the sake of satirical comedy, the play will make us think as well as laugh.

The Country Wife has three nicely related plots. Its opening lines introduce the first, in which the rakish Horner pretends to be a eunuch, fools Sir Jaspar Fidget and Lady Squeamish, and so manages to have sex with Lady Fidget and probably Mrs Dainty Fidget and Mrs Squeamish as well. This 'virtuous gang, as they call themselves' (V.ii. 96) finally returns to Horner's lodgings and boasts of having had him. In the second plot, the country wife comes to town and wants to enjoy all its pleasures, especially that of being loved by Horner; her husband, Pinchwife, knows nothing of the feigned impotence, does all he can to be avoid being cuckolded, but only makes sure that he is. In the third plot, Horner's friend Harcourt successfully woos Pinchwife's sister, Alithea, away from her proposed husband, Sparkish.

It is all over in a few hours in the theatre, and is supposed to be all over in two days in real life. The first three Acts take place on the first day, and the last two on the second. The first Act is set at Horner's lodgings late in the morning (I.i. 97–8). The second is set at Pinchwife's house early in the afternoon (most people are about to go to a play). The third begins there early in the evening (the play is over) and moves to the New Exchange a little later (the shops are still open). Now, in a modern production, we expect the interval. The fourth Act begins at Pinchwife's house on the morning of the next day (Alithea is preparing for her marriage to Sparkish before noon). The scene changes to Horner's lodgings early in the afternoon (the marriage is supposed to have taken place, and Sparkish invites people to dinner). Scenes between the Pinchwifes proceed simultaneously, and by Act V it is evening (candles are needed). The scene at Covent Garden takes place in semi-darkness ('*Enter* ALITHEA *following a torch*', V.iii.23). The final scene takes place at night, when Horner has bedded Mrs Pinchwife, though it is not too late for everybody to come to his lodgings for various reasons.[9] Obviously, the long scenes of the first three acts and the short ones of the last two create an impression of events rushing to a climax. Less obviously, the effect of the play beginning at Horner's lodgings, moving to Pinchwife's

[9] For a more detailed time and scene plan, see Judith Milhous and Robert D. Hume, *Producible Interpretation* (Southern Illinois University Press, 1985), pp. 104–6.

house and other locations, and ending back at Horner's is to suggest that the Horner plot is primary, the Pinchwife plot is secondary, and the Harcourt-Alithea-Sparkish plot is anywhere or nowhere.

The Country Wife has been and remains controversial. In its time it has been admired as a satire or farce, condemned as an immoral or frivolous play, and admired again as a serious work of dramatic art. Modern critics have wanted to show that it has unity – unity being the one criterion of merit that is generally accepted – so they have identified central themes: female hypocrisy, true and false masculinity, human folly in general, to name only three. Disagreements between these critics can perhaps be settled by arguing that such themes are all present, but none is absolutely central; yet more serious disagreements remain over attitudes to Horner. Is he the satire's hero and vehicle, or its villain and target? Is he the man we dream we could be or could have, or the man we fear we really are or have got? And unfortunately answers to these questions do not fully resolve others, such as how sorry we can feel for the Pinchwifes, or how happy for the Harcourts.[10]

But it is best to begin with Horner. He plans to fool everybody, especially the husbands, keepers, and guardians of attractive women; and to seduce the women, foreseeing that those who are disgusted by a eunuch will be fascinated by a rake. His assistant, Quack, thinks the scheme crazy, and we may think there are not many men who would sacrifice all public respect for such private satisfactions. He cannot even confide in his friends Harcourt and Dorilant. They discuss the relative merits of mistresses and fellowship, and Horner comes to the memorable conclusion:

> For my part I will have only those glorious, manly pleasures of being very drunk and very slovenly.   (I.i. 206–7)

But this is thoroughly disingenuous; he does not mean to confine himself to those pleasures, and really associates slovenliness with the miseries of marriage (ll. 315–6). When Sparkish comes to mock Homer's impotence,

---

[10] The history of Wycherley criticism in general is surveyed by B. Eugene McCarthy, *William Wycherley: A Reference Guide* (G.K. Hall, 1985), and of *Country Wife* criticism in particular by Milhous and Hume (note 9). Critics who have identified central themes include Kenneth Muir, *The Comedy of Manners* (Hutchinson, 1970): 'the main force of Wycherley's satire is directed against female hypocrisy' (p. 76); David M. Vieth, 'Wycherley's *The Country Wife:* An Anatomy of Masculinity', *Papers on Language and Literature,* vol. 2 (1966), 335–50; and R. Edgley, 'The Object of Literary Criticism', *Essays in Criticism,* vol. 14 (1964), 221–36: 'the direct topic of criticism in *The Country Wife* is folly'. Milhous and Hume conclude that, 'given the wide-open nature of the script, and the broad range of production concepts appropriate to it, to imagine that there is a single "valid" interpretation is madness' (p. 104).

his friends combine to mock Sparkish's witlessness, but they do not know that the impotence is feigned. So our first impression of Horner – and first impressions are vital in the theatre – is that he is with the wits but not of them, not only clever and cynical, but also detached and sinister.

And yet we should not be determined to prove Horner a villain, as there are no real villainies for him to commit. His first victim, Sir Jaspar Fidget, is sometimes seen as 'Wycherley's portrait of a new brand of business entrepreneur'.[11] I wish he were, but the truth is that the 'business' that busies him is at court; on his first appearance he is on the way to a Privy Council meeting, or wants to give that impression (I.i. 98), and later he says he has been 'advancing a certain project to his majesty' (III.ii. 69). As his name implies, he is 'a fidgeting, busy, dogmatical, hot-headed fop', the character of 'a politic wit' in *Love in a Wood*, and a descendant of Sir Politick Would-be in *Volpone*,[12] not a new brand of businessman at all. Both Sir Jaspar and Sir Politick are obsessed with their projects and neglectful of their wives, though only Sir Jaspar is cuckolded, and he is soon persuaded that he has not been. We do not grudge Horner the satisfaction of duping this pompous fool.

It is debatable whether the virtuous gang are Horner's victims, or *vice-versa*. At first Lady Fidget and Dainty seem comic characters like Sir Jaspar; as they find Horner's pretence of misogyny bad enough, but that of impotence even worse, they begin to prove him right in thinking that women who show an aversion to him really love the sport. Then, for an episode in Act II which is not required by the plot, the gang is joined by Mrs Squeamish, turns out in full force against Pinchwife, and drives him from his own reception room. Lady Fidget leads this outrageous assembly in revealing the lusts behind the cloak of virtue:

> To report a man has had a person, when he has not had a person, is the greatest wrong in the whole world that can be done to a person. (II. i.386–8)

Sir Jaspar re-introduces Horner, who now feels he knows Lady Fidget well enough to 'venture with her, my secret for hers' (ll. 542–3). The exchange made, she anticipates the greatest good in her whole world, to have it reported that a man has not had a person, when he has:

> But, poor gentleman, could you be so generous, so truly a man of honour, as for the sakes of us women of honour, to cause yourself to be reported no man? No man! And to suffer yourself the greatest shame that

[11] W.R. Chadwick, *The Four Plays of William Wycherley* (Mouton, 1975), p. 105
[12] See the notes on 'Persons in the Play' (p. 4) and on I.i.115, 116.

could fall upon a man, that none might fall upon us women by your
conversation? (ll. 554–59)

Her idea is that a man's greatest shame would be to be reported as a eunuch,
and his greatest triumph not to be suspected as a lecher. It is expressed in
a mixture of courtly language and sexual suggestion that soon produces
comic effects:

HORNER
I desire to be tried only, madam.
LADY FIDGET
Well, that's spoken again like a man of honour; all men of honour
desire to come to the test. (ll. 563–5)

When she comes to his lodgings to bring him to the test she takes the ini-
tiative with a pun on his name and her favourite word – 'Well, Horner, am
I not a woman of honour?' (IV.iii.38) – and holds her own in the inevitable
verbal fencing:

HORNER
To talk of honour in the mysteries of love is like talking of heaven or the
deity in an operation of witchcraft, just when you are employing the
devil; it makes the charm impotent.
LADY FIDGET
Nay, fie, let us not be smutty. (ll. 46–50)

Critics who suppose she cannot see the funny side of such remarks credit
her with no sense of humour. When Sir Jaspar interrupts, she takes control; she contrives to have sex with Horner under her husband's nose, to
re-enter with a piece of china or phallic symbol,[13] and to express satisfaction without being smutty:

LADY FIDGET
I have been toiling and moiling for the prettiest piece of china, my dear.
HORNER
Nay, she has been too hard for me, do what I could. (ll. 187–9)

Here Mrs Squeamish decides 'I'll have some china too'. We have been told
at the opening of the scene that people like Sir Jaspar and old Lady

[13] See the note on IV.iii. 204.

Squeamish think Horner 'as unfit for love as they are', but their wives, sisters, and daughters know better; so we should expect Dainty Fidget and Mrs Squeamish to want their share of him. The famous china scene is funny however it is played, but funniest I think assuming only Sir Jaspar does not know what they are talking about:

SQUEAMISH

Good Master Horner, don't think to give other people china, and me none. Come in with me too.

HORNER

Upon my honour I have none left now . . . This lady had the last there.

LADY FIDGET

Yes indeed, madam, to my certain knowledge he has no more left.

SQUEAMISH

Oh, but it may be he may have some you could not find.

LADY FIDGET

What, d'ye think if he had any left, I would not have had it too? For we women of quality never think we have china enough.

(ll. 190–202)

But soon Horner is promising china to Mrs Squeamish 'another time', Lady Fidget is taking a jealous interest in their conversation, and his explanation that Mrs Squeamish 'has an innocent, literal understanding' (l. 207) does not convince.[14]

The final appearance of the virtuous gang is another scene which is necessary for the satire rather than the plot. By Act V they have made Horner's lodgings their hideout, and he has to drink with them with a vengeance. Inspired by the wine, they acknowledge that their virtue is a disguise:

Our reputation! Lord, why should you not think that we women make use of our reputation, as you men of yours, only to deceive the world with less suspicion? Our virtue is like the statesman's religion, the Quaker's word, the gamester's oath, and the great man's honour – but to cheat those that trust us. (V.iv. 102–7)

This speech outgoes Horner in cynicism. Critics have felt that the drunken women are so disgusting that the focus of satire shifts from their affectations to their beastliness,[15] and there is certainly something alarming about

---

[14] See the note on IV.iii. 205–7.

[15] Especially Rose A. Zimbardo, *Wycherley's Drama: A Link in the Development of English Satire* (Yale, 1965), pp. 147–53

them in this mood. But a major effect of the scene is the embarrassment of Horner, who never expected anything like it. He finds himself obliged to confess the beastliness of his own activities:

> Ceremony in love and eating is as ridiculous as in fighting. Falling on briskly is all should be done on those occasions.　　　　(ll. 88–90)

Love means sex, and they all know that sex means falling on briskly. Lady Fidget immediately says women 'think wildness in a man as desirable a quality as in a duck or rabbit' (ll. 97–8). Yet she claims Horner as her own, so Mrs Squeamish and Dainty Fidget claim him too. The gang who first affected virtue, then discussed sex in code, now make plausible claims that they have all had it with Horner. And in the bedroom there is Mrs Pinchwife, who will soon escape and try to tell everyone he is hers. A man who has apparently had four women in one day can hardly avoid being an object of ridicule himself.

Another comic aspect of Horner's situation is that he can attract cuckolds and women without pretending to be a eunuch. Jack Pinchwife is an old rake who has married a country girl because, as he admits, 'I could never keep a whore to myself (I.i. 407–8). He thinks he can keep his wife to himself by locking her up or threatening violence. If he sometimes seems a clown, he often seems a tyrant; to modern audiences he will probably seem a monster. Unlike Sir Jaspar, he knows nothing of the feigned impotence and has no project to employ Horner; but he is strangely attracted to him, appearing at his lodgings for no reason, arousing his interest in Mrs Pinchwife despite himself. He feels fated to play the cuckold's part, and is grimly aware that cuckolds 'are generally makers of their own fortune' (III.i. 58–9). Those who have read their Freud[16] will see him as a neurotic character, his own worst enemy, and pathetic if you think about him. Certainly the inner life of such a man must be a mess, but Pinchwife is given few chances to win sympathy. Typically, when he threatens to murder his wife she scarcely takes him seriously, and Sparkish enters to make a joke of it (IV.iv. 42–9). Perhaps at the end, struggling for his own peace of mind to believe he has not been cuckolded, he is a sad case.

Margery Pinchwife's naïveté is so exaggerated in the early scenes that she seems a caricature of the country innocent. She twice says she has no idea what jealousy is, treats her monstrous husband as if he were a child, and seems to think him capable only of petty nastiness. Her simplicity gives her charm, however, so she can be seen as showing there are better ways of behaving than those of the town, or as being corrupted by the town's

---

[16] For example Norman Holland, *The First Modern Comedies* (Harvard, 1959), pp. 73–5

values. With the help of her mad husband and her artful maid she finds her way to Horner's bed, but naïvely supposes they can get rid of her husband and live together, and is therefore ready to tell everyone they are lovers. Has she learnt nothing at all? Well, she has ceased to long for the country, and has learned to 'loathe, nauseate, and detest' her husband (IV.iv.24). Her marriage is plainly no joke, and it may be that at the end of the play the comic balance is best preserved if she seems to have at least some hope of diversion. What does Dorilant tell her that keeps her quiet? He for his part is finally more impressed by the bad example of the Pinchwifes than by the good one of Harcourt and Alithea, so he resolves not to marry; but perhaps he has resolved to keep Mrs Pinchwife.

Harcourt and Alithea's marriage can be said to show a better way of life than Horner and Dorilant's rakish careers.[17] Alithea's critical attitude to the Pinchwifes' marriage establishes her as a sensible character, though she is herself betrothed to Sparkish. This foppish courtier and would-be wit 'can no more think the men laugh at him than that women jilt him, his opinion of himself is so good' (I.i. 211–2). Alithea is not unaware of his failings but remains faithful, trying to believe his toleration of Harcourt proves his love for her. He is certainly no Pinchwife, but only because he thinks jealousy unfashionable and finds her unattractive. Harcourt's intrigues delay the proposed marriage till other intrigues prevent it; having seen the letter Alithea is supposed to have sent to Horner, Sparkish rounds on her:

> I never had any passion for you till now, for now I hate you. 'Tis true I might have married your portion, as other men of parts of the town do sometimes; and so your servant. And to show my unconcernedness, I'll come to your wedding and resign you with as much joy as I would a stale wench to a new cully. (V.iii. 69–75)

So Sparkish's nasty nature is glimpsed behind his engaging foppery. The way is almost open for Alithea to marry Harcourt, but first he must prove himself a true lover. After all, he belongs to what she calls the society of the wits, and can talk like a libertine:

> Mistresses are like books; if you pore upon them too much they doze you and make you unfit for company, but if used discreetly you are the fitter for conversation by 'em. (I.i. 186–8)

[17] An interpretation proposed by Holland (note 16) and supported with reservations by Anne Righter, 'William Wycherley', *Restoration Theatre*, ed. John Russell Brown and Bernard Harris (Arnold, 1965), pp. 70–91

Worse, he habitually confuses courting Alithea with procuring a mistress, as in this aside about taking advantage of Sparkish:

> So we are hard put to't, when we make our rival our procurer; but . . . when all's done, a rival is the best cloak to steal to a mistress under.　　　　　　　　　　　　　　　　　　　　　　　(III.ii. 187–90)

Maybe she is right to fear that all men of the town make bad husbands. She deduces from Pinchwife's case that they are prone to jealousy and so to incarcerating their wives in the country, a fate almost worse than death (IV.i. 56–67). She sees through Harcourt's intrigues and finds his love ridiculous and troublesome (ll. 141, 145). So there is some excuse for the episode in Act V where Horner, trying to keep Pinchwife in the dark, pretends there really is something between himself and Alithea. She cannot clear her name, so Harcourt steps forward:

> Madam . . . you shall now see 'tis possible for me to love too, without being jealous. I will not only believe your innocence myself, but make all the world believe it.　　　　　　　　　　　　　　　　　　(V.iv. 262–5)

If we like, we can say they are now well matched, as she appreciates his superiority to Sparkish in both wit and worth, and he supports his romantic talk with a chivalrous gesture.

But probably we will feel more critical. As Sparkish is at best a fool, how can Alithea be both sensible about life and serious about him? It is absurd to prefer Sparkish merely because Harcourt unsettles her wedding plans; indeed worse than absurd, as Lucy points out:

> Can there be a greater cheat or wrong done to a man than to give him your person without your heart? I should make a conscience of it.　　　　　　　　　　　　　　　　　　　　　　　　　　(IV.i. 19–21)

Her brother thinks she wants Sparkish because she loves all the follies of the town; it may be worrying to have Pinchwife on our side, but we may well notice that her final acceptance of Harcourt does not dissociate her from town values, that she originally took Horner of all people for a man of honour (V.iv. 250–1), and that even when she knows what he is she urbanely supports the efforts to whitewash him. 'Come brother', she says to Pinchwife, 'your wife is yet innocent you see' (l. 394). But above all what makes the Harcourt-Alithea-Sparkish plot unacceptable as the play's moral centre is that the other plots put it in the shade. And it is no good saying moral heroes and heroines are always outshone by immoral ones. Alithea and Harcourt might have been given the positive significance of Millamant and Mirabel in *The Way of the World;* but they have not, because Wycherley was a more sceptical writer than Congreve.

Would a Restoration audience have been more inclined than we are to accept Alithea uncritically? They would have been less likely to find her attitude to town and country unbalanced. And they would have been more aware of the predicament of young unmarried women at the time: they were expected to take the husbands their parents or guardians chose for them. Pinchwife has accepted Sparkish's offer to take Alithea off his hands for £5000. The advice given to women in such a situation was to make the best of it; which perhaps is what Alithea tries to do, even hoping love will follow marriage, though Lucy puts her right here (IV.i. 23–7). Of course Wycherley knew these arranged marriages often worked badly, so we can infer that he was attacking them. And of course the Pinchwife and Fidget marriages are deplorable, so the satire on the whole institution by Horner and the wits is understandable. Still, the alternative is represented not by an admirable marriage but by a farcical courtship; compared with Millamant and Mirabel, Alithea and Harcourt tell us nothing about what the marriage of true minds might be like.

The effect, and surely also the point, of juxtaposing these three plots is to suggest that foolish or vicious men always lose their women to intelligent or virtuous ones. The foolish or vicious men – and women, as Wycherley throws in Old Lady Squeamish at the end – should present few problems for directors, audiences, or even critics. Broad similarities are clear. Sir Jaspar, believing Horner impotent and Lady Fidget virtuous, makes them companions and is cuckolded. Pinchwife, believing Horner lecherous and Margery naïve, brings them together by trying to keep them apart, and he is cuckolded too. Sparkish, believing Harcourt his friend and Alithea his property, shows her off to him and is jilted. All three fail to see that their women are capable of independent thought and action; hence these foolish or vicious men are almost wholly objects of satire. Of course there are interesting differences. Sir Jaspar is silly, harmless, and self-assured, where Pinchwife and Sparkish are relatively shrewd, vicious, and vulnerable. These two are to be contrasted, the one madly jealous and the other madly complaisant. Sparkish is engaging enough till his vicious streak appears in his showdown with Alithea. Pinchwife's real feelings are always near the surface, inclining him to violence. He may seem fated to be a cuckold, and in that way sympathetic; but the possibility of perverse and vicarious satisfactions in his role is suggested, as it is more comically in the case of Old Lady Squeamish. She actually makes her daughter kiss Horner, and thrills at the thought of debauchery: 'Oh thou harloting harlotry! Hast thou done't then?' (V.iv. 320).

The intelligent or virtuous men do present problems. Some critics want Horner to be a Lawrentian life-force and prophet of the permissive society. Others make the obvious comparison with Harcourt, to conclude that Horner is vice and Harcourt is virtue.[18] The two heroes undoubtedly differ from their dupes, and perhaps from Dorilant too, in knowing that women cannot be treated as objects. Dorilant entertains, or is entertained by, straightforward male chauvinism:

> A mistress should be like a little country retreat near the town; not to dwell in constantly, but only for a night and away, to taste the town the better when a man returns.   (I.i. 189–91)

Horner is likewise for keeping a mistress against supporting a wife, but he is interested in intelligent women and stable relationships:

> Methinks wit is more necessary than beauty; and I think no young women ugly that has it, and no handsome woman agreeable without it.   (ll. 371–3)
>
> Women . . . are like soldiers, made constant and loyal by good pay rather than by oaths and covenants.   (ll. 410–1)

And by good pay he means good sex. Harcourt romantically favours marriage against keeping; indeed he holds what remains today the most widely accepted idea of the good life. But the comparison between the two men is not exactly in his favour. Harcourt is less witty and amusing; and some of the respect he wins for his romantic idealism he loses through his farcical intrigue. He does not think his friend vicious; and neither should we. Horner commits no rapes or heartless seductions, but merely accepts the women who keep coming. The virtuous gang can even be seen as taking advantage of him. His most serious mistake is to suppose Margery Pinchwife will share his uncomplicated view of sex; this leads to more embarrassments in Act V. His most serious limitation is to live in a world of his own. He has respect for his friends, but cannot confide in them; he will do what he can to help Harcourt win Alithea, but if necessary he will fight him and injure

---

[18] For enthusiastic responses to Horner see C.D. Cecil, 'Libertine and *Précieux* Elements in Restoration Comedy', *Essays in Criticism*, vol. 9 (1959), 239–53, and Virginia Ogden Birdsall, *Wild Civility* (Indiana University Press, 1970): Horner represents 'the life force triumphant' (p. 156). For the idea that Harcourt and Horner represent right and wrong behaviour, see Holland (note 16) and Righter (note 17).

her, to protect his own secret amours. In the end he may well strike us as a man for whom sex has become a ridiculous obsession.

Critics who like neat oppositions of vice and virtue will also find them among the women. Perhaps the neatest idea is that Lady Fidget is vice, Alithea is virtue, and Margery is the happy medium.[19] But Lady Fidget and Alithea are not wholly dissimilar. They are both town women and they both talk a lot about honour; they differ in the degree to which they allow it to influence their lives, Lady Fidget superficially and Alithea excessively. Lady Fidget's hypocrisy almost insinuates her into an affair with Horner, while Alithea's honour almost traps her into a marriage with Sparkish. Alithea is saved by her own good sense, the persistence of Harcourt, and the accidental exposure of Sparkish. Lady Fidget is thwarted by her own extravagance, the fickleness of Horner, and the drunken confessions of the virtuous gang. She has to share him with them. Compared with the town ladies, Margery lacks the dubious advantages of sophisticated education, and offers the real attractions of animal vitality. But she is no happy medium; she understands only her own feelings, conspicuously not those of her husband or her lover. At the end, a semblance of order is restored when the gang and Alithea make out that nobody has been cuckolded, but Margery, having learnt something of intrigue but nothing of discretion, would blurt out the truth but for Dorilant's intervention. As Lady Fidget says – aside to Horner – 'This you get, and we too, by trusting your secret to a fool' (V.iv. 388–9).

The play, like others in the Jonsonian tradition of satirical comedy, does not so much recommend some modes of behaviour and denounce others as reveal what life is like and leave us to draw our own conclusions. And the life *The Country Wife* reveals is not unfamiliar. The world has its full complement of fools like Sir Jaspar, Sparkish, and Pinchwife; they may not be merely ridiculous, but they cannot be sympathetic, as their attitudes to women are so deplorable. The women are not such fools, though most of them are so repressed by convention or force that when they break loose they will stop at nothing to have sex. Horner accepts this situation realistically and plays the Don Juan. We may say that despite his realism he does not avoid becoming an object of satire himself; but we must admit that he gets away with it. The ideas that, like Volpone, he is becoming no more than his name implies and needs 'new tricks' to retain an interest in life keep coming to mind; but the alternative ideas, that he is an engaging scamp, or even a man with a philosophy from whom something is to be learned, will

---

[19] Birdsall (note 18) makes Margery the 'heroine' because she is neither idealistic like Alithea nor hypocritical like Lady Fidget, but 'on the side of the instincts' (pp. 147–50).

not go away. No doubt some women are more balanced than Horner's, so some happy marriages are possible, though the marriages we see in the play, those of the Fidgets and Pinchwifes, mix farce and tragedy. If we can suppose that the romantic marriage of Harcourt and Alithea will succeed, and that the lively improvisations of Horner and Margery will continue, our final impression will not be wholly pessimistic, though it may be purely personal.

<h2 style="text-align:center">Sources</h2>

Wycherley's most obvious debts are to Molière's *L'École des Maris* (1661) and *L'École des Femmes* (1662).[20] These comedies focus on the madness of men who will base marriage on the ignorance and servility of women; hence they are sources for the Pinchwife plot in particular.

In *L'École des Maris* the brothers Sganarelle and Ariste want to marry their wards, the sisters Isabelle and Léonor; Sganarelle's repressive treatment of Isabelle alienates her, but Ariste's liberal attitude towards Léonor wins her affection. Isabelle manages to convince Sganarelle that she loves him while making him her go-between with her lover, Valére. Sganarelle decides to marry her immediately, so she pretends Léonor has an assignation with Valére, and passes herself off as her sister; Sganarelle thinks he can now show Ariste the folly of liberality, and arranges the marriage of Valére and the supposed Léonor. But the real Léonor declares her love for Ariste, and when he sees what has happened Sganarelle can only 'renonce à jamais, à ce sexe trompeur'.

For *The Country Wife* Wycherley borrows the general idea of comparing repressive and liberal attitudes to women, but neither Pinchwife's repression nor Sparkish's liberality has the desired effect. He also borrows the particular device of making the victim the go-between. Isabelle tricks Sganarelle first into giving Valère a hint of her feelings, then into taking him a love letter, and finally into arranging their marriage. The Pinchwife plot develops similarly, but Margery is not as clever as Isabelle, and Pinchwife is more the victim of his own madness than Sganarelle. Isabelle's pretence that she is Léonor, to get into Valère's house, and her later apology to her sister (III.ix. 1–2), probably suggested Margery's pretence that she is Alithea, to get into Horner's lodging, and her later apology to her sister-in-law (V.iv. 295). Two further borrowings are worth noting. The sensible advice of Léonor and her servant, Lisette, to Sganarelle against his repressive behaviour (I.ii. 133–60) probably inspired that of Alithea to Pinchwife against his

[20] In Molière, *Oeuvres Complètes* (note 8), vol. 2

(II.i. 37–55), though Molière has set speeches where Wycherley has lively dialogue. And the scene in which Isabelle uses *double entendre* to deceive Sganarelle and assure Valère of her love (II.ix) broadly resembles episodes between Alithea, Harcourt, and Sparkish (II.i and III.ii), though in these Harcourt is the master of ambiguity, Sparkish is deceived, and Alithea is not wholly assured.

Wycherley's debts to *L'École des Femmes* are greater. In this play Arnolphe, a middle-aged man famous for his ridicule of cuckolds, plans to avoid being cuckolded himself by marrying his ward, Agnes, a girl he has brought up in a convent in complete ignorance. But she is so ignorant that she has no sense of obligation to him, and falls in love with Horace, the son of his friend Oronte. Although the lovers innocently confide in Arnolphe himself, he cannot prevent their eventual marriage. Again the main point of the play is the folly and wickedness of trying to achieve marriage by force.

Wycherley has of course borrowed two central characters, the girl who is innocent of the world but has a natural desire for love, and the older man who is insecure and hence possessive. But he has abandoned the convent in favour of the simple country upbringing, and the betrothed ward in favour of the girl trapped in marriage. Again there are some smaller debts and verbal echoes. Like Arnolphe, Pinchwife believes men should rule their wives, and so prefers a simple country girl to a smart town woman. The scene in which Margery arouses and allays Pinchwife's jealousy with her innocent prattle (IV.ii) derives from the similar one between Agnes and Arnolphe (II.v.). Here Molière for once indulges in innuendo; Arnolphe wants to know what Horace has taken from Agnes, fearing it is her virginity, when it is in fact her ribbon. Wycherley has a somewhat more salacious version of this incident when Pinchwife torments himself with the idea of Horner's 'beastliness' and Margery describes exactly how he kissed her. Margery's letter to Horner somewhat resembles Agnes's to Horace, but Wycherley borrows the idea of the go-between from *L'École des Maris*, and greatly expands the farcical possibilities of the episode. Broadly, then, Arnolphe, Agnes, and Horace are like Pinchwife, Margery, and Horner. But where Arnolphe is credible and pathetic, Pinchwife is melodramatic and ridiculous. Agnes is a sensible girl, who makes a conventional marriage to Horace, and becomes a less interesting character; Margery is a wild creature, who runs after Horner, and remains attractive. Compared with Horner, Horace is a colourless character; he wants marriage and gets it, but Horner wants women and gets them.

So comparisons with Molière finally emphasise differences between the two dramatists. Molière favours set speeches in couplets, Wycherley racy dialogue in prose. Indeed Molière's plays have an almost mathematical elegance, as they present data, work out possibilities, and demonstrate conclusions. Wycherley's play is equally well constructed but more complicated, and it is hard to say what is concluded. Such differences lead at least one critic to describe Wycherley as a wholly cynical writer;[21] that is a mistake, but elements of cynicism, satire, farce, and bawdy remain to be considered. If they are not simply Wycherley's own, they must have other sources.

Wycherley would surely know Terence's *The Eunuch* (161 BC)[22] – most educated men did, having been introduced to Terence at school – and could have borrowed directly from it. The play is set in Athens, and has two plots. In the first, the lovesick Phaedria and the braggart Thraso woo the courtesan Thais; in the end Phaedria gets the girl, and accepts Thraso as an exploitable hanger-on. In the second, Phaedria's brother Chaerea gets disguised as a eunuch and ravishes the supposed slave-girl Pamphila; but her brother, the countryman Chremes, proves she is a free-born Athenian, so Chaerea can marry her. The first plot is rather like that between Harcourt, Sparkish, and Alithea, and the structural relationship between Phaedria and Chaerea is rather like that between Harcourt and Horner. The second plot is not unlike that between Horner, Margery, and Pinchwife; but Chaerea is only a young scamp, Pamphila only a sex object, and Chremes only an outsider. Above all, it is not Horner's pretence of being a eunuch that enables him to have sex with Margery. *The Eunuch* also features clever servants of both sexes, but Wycherley could have derived Quack and Lucy from other classical or neo-classical sources. Where Wycherley resembles Terence more than Molière is in his cavalier cynicism about aspects of his characters' behaviour which agitate Puritan moralists.

Of course Wycherley need not have gone back to Terence for a sophisticated approach to moral issues. There was also the example of the Jonsonian comedy of humours, with its simplified characterisation, farcical elements, and satirical purpose. Wycherley was especially indebted to *Volpone*, I think, for plot devices and verbal echoes. In one episode, Volpone lusts after Celia, whose fearful husband, Corvino, keeps her locked up. She is virtuous but susceptible, and when she gives Volpone her handkerchief Corvino threatens her with his sword. Volpone feigns a fatal illness, and Corvino is persuaded that he will be made Volpone's heir if he will bring his wife to him. Some parallels are clear: Horner, like Volpone, is a monomaniac who will do anything to get what he wants; Pinchwife, like

---

[21] John Wilcox, *The Relation of Molière to Restoration Comedy* (Columbia University Press, 1938), pp. 93–4, 103

[22] In *Terence*, with an English translation by John Sargeaunt (Loeb Library), vol.1, pp. 231–351

Corvino, is a ridiculous and deplorable character who deserves to be cuckolded; Margery, like Celia, is not entirely innocent. Pinchwife tells Margery 'be sure you come not within three strides of the window' (IV.ii. 200–1), just as Corvino tells Celia he will chalk a line beyond which she must not go 'some two or three yards' from the window (II.v. 50–3). Corvino then has the ludicrous idea that he will restrain his wife by making her do everything backwards, leading him to the unintentionally obscene 'no pleasure / That thou shalt know, but backwards'. This is echoed not by Pinchwife but by the more broadly comic cuckold Sir Jaspar Fidget when he warns his wife that Horner 'is coming into you the back way' (IV.iii. 132–3). Sir Jaspar and Lady Fidget descend from Jonson's Sir Politick and Lady Would-be, the two gentlemen hoping to impress the state's rulers with their projects, and the two ladies able to embarrass the play's heroes with their attentions.

STAGE HISTORY

The Country Wife was first performed, probably on 12 January 1675, by the King's Company at the Theatre Royal, Drury Lane. This was a new building designed by Sir Christopher Wren, looking in some ways forward to our modern theatres, in others back to the Elizabethan. Like our theatres it was roofed over and needed illumination, but like the Elizabethan it had a large open forestage reaching well into the auditorium. Access to this main acting area was by a pair of doors at either side; a stage direction such as '*Exit* HORNER *at t'other door*' (IV.iii. 131) means Horner goes out at the other door on the same side. Behind the forestage was the proscenium arch, and behind that a large recess where scenes were mounted and changed. The recess was dimly lit compared with the rest of the theatre, and the scenes would give only general impressions of the different locales, thus not greatly distracting attention from the actors on the forestage. After the prologue a green curtain was raised to reveal the first scene, but later scene changes were made in view of the audience. Here is an early description of the auditorium:

> The pit is an amphitheatre, filled with benches without backboards, and adorned and covered with green cloth. Men of quality, particularly the younger sort, some ladies of reputation and virtue, and an abundance of damsels that hunt for prey, sit all together in this place, higgledy-piggledy, chatter, toy, play, hear, hear not. Further up, against the wall, under the first gallery, and just opposite to the stage, rises another amphitheatre, which is taken up by persons of the best quality, among whom are generally very few men. The galleries, whereof there

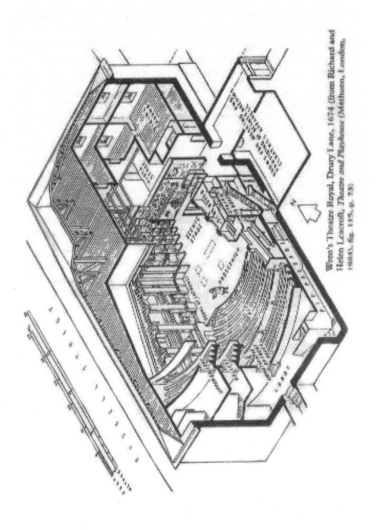

Wren's Theatre Royal, Drury Lane, 1674 (from Richard and Helen Leacroft, *Theatre and Playhouse* (Methuen, London, 1984), fig. 115, p. 73)

are only two rows, are filled with none but ordinary people, particularly in the upper one.[23]

The amphitheatre for 'persons of the best quality' was divided into boxes. At the time of the first performance of *The Country Wife* the theatre could have been more dominated by the court than this description suggests, especially if the King favoured it with his presence in the royal box, or the court wits with their comments from the pit. The precise capacity is uncertain, but it can be calculated that the theatre would not seem overcrowded till the audience approached a thousand, and that a performance would remain profitable till it fell below five hundred. So this theatre, though grander than the Elizabethan, remained intimate.

The King's Company was well established and had some experienced players. No doubt they were versatile, but they probably played to their strengths, and Wycherley must have written parts with particular actors and actresses in mind. In any case regular playgoers, recognising the players, would see new roles through memories of old ones – an effect familiar enough today on television and in the cinema. So to understand Wycherley's intentions or the effect *The Country Wife* probably produced, it is vital to know something of the original players.[24] The male leads were Charles Hart as Horner and Edward Kynaston as Harcourt; they had already played against each other as a rake and a romantic in Wycherley's *Love in a Wood*. As Hart was a man of forty-five who had played many major roles in comedy and tragedy, his Horner would have been masterful if potentially dissipated; as Kynaston was young enough to have played women's roles immediately after the Restoration, his Harcourt would have been attractive if potentially effeminate. The comic victims were played by two elderly actors, Michael Mohun and William Cartwright, and by young Joseph Haines. Mohun was probably best known for playing tragic villains such as Volpone and Iago, and Cartwright for comic characters such as Falstaff and Corbaccio, so Mohun's Pinchwife would probably be alarming as well as funny, and Cartwright's Sir Jaspar a more straightforwardly comic figure. Haines was a song and dance man, already famous for

---

[23] M. Misson's *Memoirs and Observations . . . Translated by Mr Ozell* (1719), pp. 219–20, quoted in *The London Stage, Part I: 1660–1700*, ed. William van Lennep, introduction by Emmett L. Avery and Arthur H. Scouten (Southern Illinois University Press, 1965), pp. xli–xlii. This introduction and the relevant parts of John Loftis, Richard Southern, Marion Jones, and A.H. Scouten, *The Revels History of Drama in English, Vol. V: 1660–1750* (Methuen, 1976) and *The London Theatre World*, ed. Robert D. Hume (Southern Illinois, 1980), are my main sources of information on the Restoration theatre.

[24] Edward A. Langhans, Philip H. Highfill, Jr., and Kalman A. Burnim, *A Biographical Dictionary of Stage Personnel in London, 1660–1800* (Southern Illinois University Press, 1973–) and correspondence with Professor Langhans are my main sources here and in the notes on the players (pp. 4–5).

eccentric behaviour both on and off the stage; his buffoonery would perhaps make a highly romantic portrayal of Harcourt and Alithea less likely. The principal women's roles were taken by Mrs Boutell as Mrs Pinchwife, Mrs Knepp as Lady Fidget, and Mrs James as Alithea. Mrs Boutell was

> low of stature, had very agreeable features, a good complexion, but a childish look. Her voice was weak, tho' very mellow; she generally acted the *young innocent lady* whom all the heroes are mad in love with; she was a favourite of the town.[25]

She often appeared in breeches roles, and no doubt looked more attractive than ever when dressed as a boy in III.ii, an effect which Pinchwife foolishly fails to anticipate. But her youth and innocence against Mohun's age and violence could have played for pathos. Certainly her ideas of what she wants and how to get it would remain pathetically vague compared with those of Mrs Knepp's Lady Fidget. Mrs Knepp was more dynamic; Pepys said she was 'the most excellent, mad-humoured thing, and sings the noblest that ever I heard', while her lover, Haines, called her 'that delicate compound of spirit and rump'. One of her earlier comic roles had been Lady Flippant in *Love in a Wood*, another woman whose code of 'honour' conveys appetite for sex, to those who can decode it. Mrs Knepp's various talents would have been put to splendid effect in the great drunken scene at Horner's lodgings. Mrs James had previously played normal but minor characters like Bianca in *Othello*; in the company of Mrs Boutell and Mrs Knepp she is unlikely to have made Alithea the central role demanded by some modern critical interpretations. It seems safe to conclude that the King's Company's performance would have avoided the extremes of pure farce and grim satire.

The evidence that the play 'was an immediate success'[26] is slight. It was acted again during the following season, there were probably revivals during the 1683–4, 1688–9 and 1694–5 seasons, and there could have been others which have not been recorded. Jeremy Collier, in his *Short View of the Immorality and Profaneness of the English Stage* (1698), mentions Wycherley's plays much less often than those of Dryden, Vanbrugh, and others, apparently not because he thought them less offensive, but because they were less popular. But during the first forty years of the eighteenth century *The Country Wife* was a stock piece, 'not tremendously popular but apparently a dependable part of the repertory'; it was especially successful from 1725 to

[25] Thomas Betterton, *History of the English Stage* (1741), p. 21; this book was apparently compiled from Betterton's notes by William Oldys and Edmund Curll.

[26] *The Country Wife*, ed. David Cook and John Swannell (The Revels Plays, 1975), p. lxiv

1742, when there were often rival productions by the two patent companies, employing the best actors and actresses. During the next decade its popularity waned, and in 1753 it was acted for the last time in its original form until the present century.[27]

The offensiveness of the play was immediately remarked on; Wycherley responds to such criticisms in a scene in *The Plain Dealer*, in which the prudish Olivia thinks no modest woman can see *The Country Wife* without blushing, though the sensible Eliza evidently can. Olivia finds 'clandestine obscenity' in the name Horner, and feels that Wycherley has 'quite taken away the reputation of poor *China* itself'. The fop Novel believes all the trouble could have been avoided if only the author had put the play into rhyme, which can make double-meanings pass with the ladies for tender passions. As the scene is an imitation of Molière's *La Critique de L'École des Femmes*, it is not clear what the criticisms of *The Country Wife* really amounted to; it is clear that Wycherley himself thought little of them. But there is some evidence, admittedly tenuous, that the impact of *The Country Wife* began to be modified quite early on. Colley Cibber records that William Mountfort, playing Sparkish some time in the late seventeenth century, gave a 'delightful instance' of his ability to play 'the brisk, vain, rude and lively coxcomb, the false, flashy pretender to wit, and the dupe of his own sufficiency'.[28] This relatively serious conception of the role could imply an attempt to give the Harcourt-Alithea-Sparkish plot greater centrality, and so in a measure moralise the play.

The effect of Collier's moralistic attack on Restoration drama can be felt in Steele's account of a benefit performance for Mrs Bicknell at Drury Lane in 1709.[29] Steele says Mrs Bicknell 'made a very pretty figure, and exactly entered into the nature of the part' of Mrs Pinchwife. He then feels he must explain the relationship of the Pinchwifes in detail, and defend Wycherley against charges of immorality. We should note Mrs Pinchwife's sad fall from grace, and the satire on Pinchwife:

> The poet on many occasions, where the propriety of the character will admit of it, insinuates that there is no defence against vice, but the contempt of it, and has, in the natural ideas of an untainted innocent, shown the gradual steps to ruin which persons of condition run into, without the help of a good education to form their conduct. The torment of a jealous coxcomb, which arises from his own false maxims, and

[27] E.L. Avery, '*The Country Wife* in the Eighteenth Century', *Research Studies*, vol. 10 (1942), 141–72, and 'The Reputation of Wycherley's Comedies as Stage Plays in the Eighteenth Century', ibid., vol. 12 (1942), 132–54

[28] *An Apology for the Life of Mr Colley Cibber* (1740), ch. 5, p. 77

[29] *The Tatler*, 16 April 1709

the aggravation of his pain, by the very words in which he sees her innocence, makes a very pleasant and instructive satire.

But Steele apparently found no sign of satire on Horner, and could only
defend Wycherley's portrayal of the rake by a historical argument:

> The character of Horner, and the design of it, is a good representation
> of the age in which the comedy was written; at which time, love and
> wenching were the business of life, and the gallant manner of pursuing
> women was the best recommendation at court. To this only is it to be
> imputed, that a gentleman of Mr Wycherley's character and sense, con-
> descends to represent the insults done to the honour of the bed, without
> just reproof.

The feelings that the language of the play was indecent, and its whole tendency
immoral, so intensified during the eighteenth century that eventually
two revised versions were made. These were John Lee's *The Country Wife*
(1765) and Garrick's *The Country Girl* (1766). Lee's version is a two-act
entertainment aimed at being 'inoffensively humorous'.[30] Horner, the feigned
impotence, and the Fidgets disappear entirely. Dorilant becomes the
would-be seducer of Mrs Pinchwife, but finally retires so that she and her
husband can try again. Alithea, now unquestionably the heroine, advises
Pinchwife to let his wife mingle in society and 'improve that mind, which has
hitherto been too un-formed to defend itself from the attacks of its own
passions, or from those of others'; that is, she advises the education that Steele
said was wanting. She also sensibly prefers Harcourt to Sparkish, and declares
that Sparkish does not really love her. Harcourt's disguise as a parson is
retained – which would not have pleased Collier – but much of Wycherley's
bawdy wit is banished. Garrick's version[31] is essentially worse than Lee's,
because although it is a five-act play, it involves a more extensive rewriting of
the original. Margery Pinchwife becomes Peggy Thrift, the country girl; Jack
Pinchwife becomes Jack Moody, her guardian, who only pretends she is his
wife. Old Horner becomes young Belville, Harcourt's nephew, and the main
plot concerns Belville and Peggy's successful endeavour to thwart her guardian
and get married. Harcourt wins Alithea from Sparkish, but her dowry has
doubled with inflation (from £5000 to £10,000), and the settings and allusions
have also been updated. It was thought that the comedy now blended 'the

---

[30] *The Country Wife, A Comedy in Two Acts* (1765), 'Advertisement', title-page, verso
[31] *The Country Girl*, in *The British Theatre . . . With Biographical and Critical Remarks* by
Mrs Inchbald (1808), vol. 16. Mrs Inchbald's 'Remarks' (p. 5) are quoted below.

witty dialogue of former times' with 'the purity, and happy incidents, of modern dramas'. Not surprisingly, Garrick's version eclipsed Lee's; it reached the New York stage in 1794, and there and in London survived to the end of the nineteenth century and even beyond. But from a modern point of view *The Country Girl* is sentimental and boring, where *The Country Wife* is astringent and provocative.

Wycherley's play returned to the London stage in 1924, when it was presented at the Regent Theatre by the Phoenix Society. The director was Montague Summers, who recalled that 'Mrs Grundy wailed aloud and wrung her mittened hands', as 'the raptured audience rocked with laughter'.[32] But the theatre critics were less enthusiastic, and the play had to wait another ten years for a fully successful professional performance. Meanwhile a production at the Everyman Theatre in 1926 should perhaps be regarded as the last gasp of *The Country Girl*, and one in New York in 1931 was apparently the first performance of *The Country Wife* in America. Then, in 1934 a production by Balliol Holloway at the Ambassadors Theatre had a run of five months and was well received by the critics, and in 1936 one by Tyrone Guthrie at the Old Vic proved beyond doubt that the play had regained its place in the repertoire. In this production Michael Redgrave was Horner, Edith Evans was Lady Fidget, and Ruth Gordon played Mrs Pinchwife with an American accent. It was perhaps not meant to suggest that all American girls were essentially naïve. Miss Gordon had already appeared in an American production of the play, and had to return to appear in another on Broadway, so although the Old Vic Company 'played to capacity every night' the run was limited. The Broadway version was less successful because the cast was comparatively lacking in 'star appeal' and 'gusto'.[33] There was only one London production during the Second World War and the period of austerity afterwards, but since 1955 there have been frequent revivals there, in the provinces, and in America. The most important were perhaps: at the Royal Theatre, Stratford, E.15, directed by Tony Richardson, in 1955; at the Royal Court, directed by George Devine, with Joan Plowright as Mrs Pinchwife, in 1956; at the Chichester Festival, directed by Robert Chetwyn, with Maggie Smith as Mrs Pinchwife and Hugh Paddick as Sparkish, in 1969; and at the National Theatre, directed by Peter Hall, with Albert Finney as Horner, in 1977. The play of course offers an unusually high proportion of good parts, and star actresses and actors have appeared as Mrs Pinchwife, Lady Fidget, Horner, Pinchwife, and Sparkish. The direction the play takes will be determined mainly by

[32] *The Playhouse of Pepys* (Routledge, 1935), pp. 318–19
[33] Tyrone Guthrie, *A Life in the Theatre* (Columbus Books, 1987), p. 165

the casting, though Hall blames himself for the relative failure of the National Theatre production.[34]

It seems the Chichester Festival production inspired the Warren Beatty film *Shampoo*, but the Old Vic production discouraged professional directors for a decade. Then came five revivals in four years: in 1990, at the Mermaid Theatre, directed by Richard Trethowan, with Fenella Fielding as Lady Fidget; in 1991, a touring production by the Cambridge Theatre Company, directed by Mike Alfreds; in 1992, at Holland Park, directed by Peter Benedict; in 1993, at the Harrogate Festival, directed by Andrew Manley, and at the Swan Theatre, Stratford-upon-Avon, by the Royal Shakespeare Company, directed by Max Stafford-Clark. Also in 1993 there was *Lust*, a musical version by the Heather brothers, at the Theatre Royal, Haymarket. All these were quite widely reviewed, if not always well received. The Mermaid revival suffered from an outbreak of flu among the players, and Ms Fielding stole what was left of the show; the Cambridge from a fit of modishness by the director, and the actors onstage competed for attention with those off. The Holland Park setting encouraged vivacious acting, gorgeous costume, and high fantasy. The three roughly concurrent versions of 1993, however, led to suggestions that the play was especially appropriate at a time when the incompetence and hypocrisy of the nation's governors and moralists had been exposed. The musical could not avoid being called a 'Restoration romp', but the Harrogate revival insisted on contemporary relevance to the extent of omitting the romantic plot. The Stratford revival came closest to the text and perhaps the spirit of the play, though it may have been too serious; according to *The Times*, 'a puritan production of a cavalier play'.

Contemporary relevance is often overdone. When the Stratford production moved to London in 1994, one reviewer could not believe the play had been so unpleasant when first performed, 'but there may be no honest alternative today', while another thought the feminist interpretation took away the fun. At the Citizen's Theatre, Glasgow, in 1997, the setting was a nightmare city of angled ramps and sliding panels, bathed in a sickly yellow and pink light, and the play became a sermon on the dangers of sexual pleasure. At the Wolsey, Ipswich, later that year, Mrs Pinchwife was a bimbo, sometimes kept in a cage, and Quack made his observations on the intercom. At the Bridewell, London, in 1999, the characters appeared on a catwalk, festooned in the latest fantasies of fashion, to the accompaniment of pounding rock music; hence our 'vain and vulnerable society' was 'painfully recognizable' (*The Independent*). Reviewers are usually ready to welcome more straightforward productions, like those at the Gatehouse, London,

---

[34] *Peter Hall's Diaries,* ed. John Goodwin (Hamish Hamilton, 1983), p. 319

in 1998, and at the Crucible, Sheffield, in 2000. The former was a 'balanced take on a play that lends itself to extremes', though the latter was 'relentlessly boisterous', better for the box office than for Wycherley's reputation as a serious dramatist. A surprising development at the Crucible was 'the Alithea/Harcourt subplot played straight' and 'as a model of potential happiness' (*The Guardian*).

In 2007–8 the play was revived at the Haymarket by the Theatre Royal Company, directed by Jonathan Kent. Twenty reviews in London papers not surprisingly expressed contradictory opinions, but most thought the production made the play seem farcical. Some characterisations were so energetically ridiculous from the outset that they could not develop; Margery was such a screaming virago that it was hard to see why Pinchwife was furiously jealous.

The Text

The Country Wife was first published in quarto in 1675 (Q1). By the standards of the time it is a nicely printed book with few errors. The impression that it could have been printed from an author's fair copy is supported by the unusually detailed stage directions.[35] The first quarto was reprinted in 1683 (Q2), and the second in 1688 (Q3) and 1695 (Q4). These reprints correct some errors but make quite a lot more. Q4 was very inaccurately reprinted in the same year (Q5).[36] Perhaps because Q4 tried to regularise the spelling and punctuation it was also the copy text for the octavo edition of Wycherley's *Works* in 1713 (O). This was the last edition in the author's lifetime. There is no evidence that he ever revised the text; if he had, presumably he would have corrected some obvious errors which survived the printing process.[37]

The copy text for this edition is the Cambridge University Library copy of Q1 (in the Brett-Smith collection), collated with the Readex microprint of the Library of Congress copy, the University Microfilms (Ann Arbor) microfilm of the Huntington Library copy, and the Scolar Press facsimile of the British Library copy. I have also examined the Cambridge University

[35] Cook and Swannell (note 25), p. lxxi. Directions which indicate more than stage business include 'ALITHEA *walks carelessly to and fro*' (III.ii.275), 'MRS PINCHWIFE *alone leaning on her elbow*' (IV.iv.i) and 'PINCHWIFE *stands doggedly, with his hat over his eyes*' (V.iv.297).

[36] Q5 has the running-title '*The Country Wife*', where Q1–4 and O have '*The Country-Wife*'. Q4 and Q5 were carefully distinguished by Robert N.E. Megaw, 'Notes on Restoration Plays (1)', *Studies in Bibliography*, vol. 3 (1951–2), 252–3, except that, as T.H. Fujimura notes in his edition of *The Country Wife* (Regents Restoration Drama Series, 1965), p. ix, Q4 is based on Q2 not Q3.

[37] See for examples IV.iii.205–7 note and V.iv.385, 388 note.

Library copies of Q2–5 and O. Departures from Q1 involving changes of wording have been recorded in the footnotes, where readings from Q2–5 and O are sometimes quoted in support. Speech prefixes have been expanded, and for the sake of clarity MR has been dropped before Pinchwife's name but MRS has been retained before his wife's. In the stage directions *Mistress* and *Mrs.* have been regularised to MRS (for Mrs Pinchwife) and *Mrs* for the other ladies, while in the text, Mr. and Mrs. have been expanded to Master and Mistress. It is hoped that these procedures will not be thought sexist. Additions to the text, mostly stage directions, are given in square brackets. Directions for asides are placed before the speeches to which they refer. Spelling and punctuation are modernised in line with New Mermaid policy. Modernising the punctuation presents both opportunities and problems; where speeches have a rhetorical structure it can often be clarified, but Q1 often employs dashes to show theatrical pauses of varying lengths. These dashes have sometimes been replaced by the punctuation we would expect from the grammar, and have sometimes been retained, to show transitions from asides to dialogue, parenthetical remarks, and unfinished sentences. I believe the text is suitable for both reading and acting, though a scholarly director bent on authenticity would doubtless make a fresh start with Q1.

FURTHER READING

As the introduction will have suggested, I think the student would do well to read sources or analogues, in translation where necessary: Terence's *The Eunuch*, Jonson's *Volpone*, Molière's *L'École des Maris* and *L'École des Femmes*. I would also recommend reading Wycherley's earlier plays and *The Plain Dealer* (ed. James L. Smith, New Mermaid, 1979), Etherege's *The Man of Mode* (ed. John Barnard, New Mermaids, 1979), and Congreve's *The Way of the World* (ed. Brian Gibbons, New Mermaid 2nd edition, 1994). Students who feel obliged to rely on secondary sources are urged to read several, and to consider the degree to which different interpretations can be reconciled.

Editions

The Complete Plays of William Wycherley, ed. Gerald Weales (New York University Press, 1967). Old spelling.

The Plays of William Wycherley, ed. Arthur Friedman (Oxford, 1979). Old spelling.

The Plays of William Wycherley, ed. Peter Holland (Cambridge, 1981). Modernised text; available in paperback.

William Wycherley: The Country Wife and Other Plays, ed. Peter Dixon (Oxford, 1996). Modernised text; paperback.

Books

Birdsall, Virginia Ogden, *Wild Civility: The English Comic Spirit on the Restoration Stage* (Indiana University Press, 1970). Three chapters on Wycherley.

Chadwick, W.R., The Four Plays of William Wycherley (Mouton 1975). Clear and comprehensive.

Gill, Pat, *Interpreting Ladies: Women, Wit, and Morality in the Restoration Comedy of Manners* (University of Georgia Press, 1994). Good chapter on Wycherley.

Harwood, John T., *Critics, Values, and Restoration Comedy* (Southern Illinois University Press, 1982). On *The Country Wife* and its critics, pp. 98–114.

Holland, Norman N., *The First Modern Comedies* (Harvard, 1959). Four chapters on Wycherley.

McCarthy, B. Eugene, *William Wycherley: A Biography* (Ohio University Press, 1979)

Milhous, Judith, and Robert D. Hume, *Producible Interpretation* (Southern Illinois University Press, 1985). Excellent chapter on *The Country Wife* and its interpreters.

Owen, Susan, *Perspectives on Restoration Drama* (Manchester University Press, 2002). Chapter on *The Country Wife* with comprehensive bibliography.

Powell, Jocelyn; *Restoration Theatre Production* (Routledge, 1984). Excellent chapter on *The Country Wife*.

Rogers, K.M., *William Wycherley* (Twayne's English Authors, 1972) An 'overview' or survey; dated on the biographical side.

Thompson, James, *Language in Wycherley's Plays* (University of Alabama Press, 1984). Chapter on 'Figurative Language in *The Country Wife*'.

Weber, Harold, *The Restoration Rake-Hero* (University of Wisconsin Press, 1986). On Horner, pp. 53–69.

Zimbardo, Rose A., *Wycherley's Drama: A Link in the Development of English Satire* (Yale, 1965)

Essays

Burke, Helen, 'Wycherley's "Tendentious Joke":The Discourse of Alterity in *The Country Wife*', *The Eighteenth Century: Theory and Interpretation*, vol. 29 (1988), 227–41. A feminist view.

Cohen, Derek, 'The Revenger's Comedy: A Reading of *The Country Wife*', *Durham University Journal*, vol. 76 (1983), 31–6

Craik, T.W., 'Some Aspects of Satire in Wycherley's Plays', *English Studies*, vol. 41 (1960), 168–79

Duncan, Douglas, 'Mythic Parody in *The Country Wife*', *Essays in Criticism*, vol. 31 (1981), 299–312. Interesting, but tough.

Edgley, R., 'The Object of Literary Criticism', *Essays in Criticism*, vol. 14 (1964), 221–36. On *The Country Wife*, 231–6

Kaufman, Anthony, 'The Shadow of the Burlador: Don Juan on the Continent and in England,' *Comedy from Shakespeare to Sheridan*, ed. A.R. Braunmuller and J.C. Bulman (Associated University Presses, 1986), pp. 229–54. Horner and other Don Juans.

Love, Harold, 'The Theatrical Geography of *The Country Wife*', *Southern Review* (Adelaide), vol. 16 (1983), 404–15

Malekin, Peter, 'Wycherley's Dramatic Skills and the Interpretation of *The Country Wife*', *Durham University Journal*, vol . 61 (1969), 32–40

Neill, Michael, 'Horned Beasts and China Oranges: Reading the Signs in *The Country Wife*', *Eighteenth Century Life*, vol. 12 (1988), 3–17

Nelson, T.G.A., 'Stooping to Conquer in Goldsmith, Haywood, and Wycherley', *Essays in Criticism*, vol. 46 (1996), 319–39. Compares *She Stoops to Conquer, Fantomina, or, Love in a Maze*, and *The Country Wife*.

Righter, Anne, 'William Wycherley', *Restoration Theatre* (Stratford-upon-Avon Studies, vol. 6; Arnold, 1965), pp. 70–91.

Thompson, Peggy, 'The Limits of Parody in *The Country Wife*, *Studies in Philology,* vol. 89 (1992), 100–14. On 'Wycherley's ambivalent approach to the myth of a sexual fall'.

Vieth, David M., 'Wycherley's *The Country Wife:* An Anatomy of Masculinity', *Papers on Language and Literature,* vol. 2 (1966), 335–50.

Reference

Hume, Robert D., 'William Wycherley: Text, Life, Interpretation', *Modern Philology,* vol. 78 (1981), 399–415. Evaluative.

McCarthy, B. Eugene, *William Wycherley: A Reference Guide* (G.K. Hall, 1985). Comprehensive; annotated.

Theatre Record, vols. 10 (1990), 1672–4; 11 (1991)–1505–6; 12 (1992), 873; 13 (1993), 930–7, 827–31; 14 (1994). 868–9; 17 (1997) 168–9,1485; 18 (1998) 1007; 19 (1999) 80; 20 (2000) 1306, 1462; 27 (2007) 1232–7. Collected reviews of the productions of those years.

ABBREVIATIONS

Cook and David Cook and John Swannell (eds.) *The*
Swanell   *Country Wife* (The Revels Plays, 1975)

Dixon   Peter Dixon (ed.), *William Wycherley: The Country Wife and Other Plays* (Oxford, 1996)

ed.   editor; in the textual notes, indicates a reading not found in Q1–5 and O.

Etherege References to *The Man of Mode* are to John Barnard's New Mermaid edition.

Farmer and J.S. Farmer and W.E. Henley, *A Dictionary of Slang*
Henley   (1890–1904; Wordsworth Editions, 1987)

Friedman Arthur Friedman (ed.), *The Plays of William Wycherley* (Oxford, 1979). References to Wycherley's Plays other than *The Country Wife* are to this edition.

Holland   Peter Holland (ed.), *The Plays of William Wycherley* (Cambridge, 1981)

Hunt   John Dixon Hunt (ed.), *The Country Wife* (New Mermaid, 1973)

Jonson   References to *Volpone* and *The Alchemist* are to *The Complete Plays of Ben Jonson*, ed. G.A. Wilkes (Oxford, 1982) vol. III.

Markley   Robert Markley, *Two-Edg'd Weapons: Style and Ideology in the Comedies of Etherege, Wycherley and Congreve* (Oxford, 1988)

O   The octavo edition of Wycherley's *Works* (1713)

OED   *Oxford English Dictionary*, 2nd. ed. (1989)

Partridge Eric Partridge, *A Dictionary of Historical Slang*, abridged by Jacqueline Simpson (Penguin, 1972)

Q1, 2, 3, 4, 5 The quarto editions of *The Country Wife* (1675, 1683, 1688, 1695); see section on 'The Text', pp. xxxvi–xxxvii.

sd   stage direction

Shakespeare   References to the plays are to *The Complete Works*, ed. Stanley Wells and Gary Taylor (Oxford, 1986).

sp   speech prefix; i.e., the name of a character prefixed to a speech

Weales   Gerald Weales (ed.), *The Complete Plays of William Wycherley* (New York University Press, 1967)

THE

Country-Wife,

A

COMEDY,

Acted at the

THEATRE ROYAL.

Written by Mr. *Wycherley.*

---

*Indignor quicquam reprehendi, non quia crassè
Compositum illepidève putetur, sed quia nuper :
Nec veniam Antiquis, sed honorem & præmia posci.*
                                                    Horat.

LONDON,

Printed for *Thomas Dring*, at the *Harrow*, at the
Corner of *Chancery-Lane* in *Fleet-street.* 1675.

[33]

Indignior some copies of Q1 (*Indignor* other copies, Q2–5, O). *Indignor* is correct.

Motto Horace, *Epistles* 2.1.76–8. Dryden quoted the first two lines in his *Of Dramatick Poesie* (1668) and mentioned Terence's *The Eunuch* as a play by an ancient writer which is not faultless. As *The Eunuch* is one of his sources, Wycherley could be implying specifically that it deserved only indulgence (*veniam*), while his own play deserved honour and rewards (*honorem & praemia*); or he could be thinking generally of ancient writers. Pope's version in the *Imitations of Horace* is:

> I lose my patience, and I own it too,
> When works are censured, not as bad, but new;
> While if our elders break all reason's laws,
> These fools demand not pardon, but applause.   (*Epistle* 2.1.115–18)

THE PERSONS

MR HORNER	*Mr Hart*
MR HARCOURT	*Mr Kynaston*
MR DORILANT	*Mr Lydall*
MR PINCHWIFE	*Mr Mohun*
MR SPARKISH	*Mr Haines*
SIR JASPAR FIDGET	*Mr Cartwright*
MRS MARGERY PINCHWIFE	*Mrs Boutell*
MRS ALITHEA	*Mrs James*
MY LADY FIDGET	*Mrs Knepp*
MRS DAINTY FIDGET	*Mrs Corbet*
MRS SQUEAMISH	*Mrs Wyatt*
OLD LADY SQUEAMISH	*Mrs Rutter*
WAITERS, SERVANTS, AND ATTENDANTS	
A BOY	
A QUACK	*Mr Shatterell*
LUCY, *Alithea's Maid*	*Mrs Corey*

The Scene: *London*

The Persons This cast list is illogically placed after the prologue in Q1 and most modern editions. It omits Clasp, a bookseller, mentioned at III.ii.159, and a parson mentioned in the stage direction at V.iv.227.

HORNER: maker of cuckolds (see I.i.83, note); the word is used in this sense by John Fletcher in *The Elder Brother* (1637) IV.iv. To Olivia in *The Plain Dealer* 'the very name' suggests 'the image of a goat, a town-bull, or a satyr' (II.i.412–15), that is, a lecherous creature. Also associated with the Devil, traditionally represented as horned, and a not uncommon English surname which occurs in the rhyme 'Little Jack Horner'. But Homer's Christian name is Harry (I.i.286), again associated with both womanisers (see V.iv.177, note) and the Devil ('Old Harry').

HARCOURT suggests an English gentleman; perhaps derived from place names m Shropshire. His Christian name is Frank (II.i.187 and elsewhere) and it may be significant that his rival Sparkish falsely claims frankness as a virtue.

DORILANT suggests *jeunesse dorée*; perhaps derived from Dorante, a common name for such characters in contemporary French drama, and a source for the name Dorimant, the rake-hero of *The Man of Mode*. Dorilant's Christian name is Dick (I.i.290 and II.i.187).

PINCHWIFE: one who restricts his wife's freedom; she expects him to 'pinch' her (IV.iii.289). His Christian name is Jack (I.i.359).

SPARKISH: a bit of a 'spark', a young man who affects smartness in dress and manners. The only major character whose Christian name is not given.

JASPAR FIDGET: name with various associations. Jaspar derives from Caspar, 'keeper of the treasure', the Magus traditionally supposed to represent the black races; its association with villains belongs to Victorian melodrama. Fidget suggests a busybody; in *Love in a Wood* 'a politic wit' is defined as 'a fidgeting, busy, dogmatical, hot-headed fop' (II.i.261), and Sir

[35]

Jaspar's 'business' is political rather than commercial (see I.i.115–16 and notes, and introduction, p. xvi).

MARGERY perhaps already suggested a sluttish country girl, like Margery Daw; see Iona and Peter Opie, *Oxford Dictionary of Nursery Rhymes* (1977) p. 298. In *The Merchant of Venice* Old Gobbo, a rustic, has a wife called Margery (II.ii.84–6).

ALITHEA: derived from the Greek word for 'truth'; a fashionable name in the seventeenth century

DAINTY: fastidious (*OED a.*5); not a true Christian name

SQUEAMISH: prudish (*OED* 7). Mrs Squeamish's Christian name may be Bridget (IV.iii.178 and note).

QUACK: boastful pretender to knowledge, especially in medicine

LUCY: derived from the Latin word for 'light'

Players

Hart, Charles (*c.* 1630–83), a sharer in the King's Company and a leading actor, famous for heroic roles, including Almanzor in Dryden's *Conquest of Granada* and several Shakespearean tragic figures. His comic roles had included Mosca in *Volpone* and Ranger in *Love in a Wood*, and he had been the lover of both Nell Gwyn and Lady Castlemaine.

Kynaston, Edward (1643–1712), a leading actor, was originally famous for women's roles, later for romantic heroes, including Valentine in *Love in a Wood*.

Lydall or Lidell, Edward (fl. 1655–77), a regular actor who did not often take major roles

Mohun, Michael (1616?–84), a sharer in the King's Company and a leading actor, whose roles had included villains and rogues: Cassius in *Julius Caesar*, Iago, Volpone, Face in *The Alchemist*, and Dapperwit in *Love in a Wood*

Haines, Joseph (1648?–1701), a young comedian, already famous for eccentricity both on and off the stage. See Kenneth M. Cameron, 'Jo Haynes, Infamis', *Theatre Notebook* vol. 24 (1969–70), 56–67.

Cartwright, William (*c.* 1604–86), a sharer in the King's Company and a leading comedian, whose roles had included Falstaff, Corbaccio in *Volpone*, and Sir Epicure Mammon in *The Alchemist*

Boutell or Bowtell, Mrs Barnaby, née Elizabeth Davenport (*c.* 1649–1715), a versatile and popular actress who had played major roles in heroic plays and tragedies and breeches roles in comedies and farces. She was small and pretty and 'generally acted the *young innocent lady* whom all the heroes are mad in love with; she was a favourite of the town' (Introduction, note 25). See Judith Milhous, 'Elizabeth Bowtell and Elizabeth Davenport: Some Problems Solved', *Theatre Notebook* vol. 39 (1985), 124–34.

James Elizabeth (fl. 1669–1703?), took mainly minor roles, including Isabel in *Love in a Wood*.

Knepp, Mrs Christopher, née Elizabeth Carpenter (fl. 1659–81), famous as both actress and singer; her comic roles had included Lady Flippant in *Love in a Wood*. See Robert Latham (ed.), *The Diary of Samuel Pepys*, vol. 10 (Bell and Hyman, 1983), pp. 215–16.

Corbet, Mary (fl. 1670?–82?), took mainly minor roles.

Wyatt, Mrs, otherwise unknown

Rutter, Margaret (fl. 1661–*c.* 1680), took mainly minor roles, including Emilia in *Othello* and Mrs Crossbite in *Love in a Wood*, 'an old cheating jilt, and bawd to her daughter'.

Shatterell, Robert (born *c.* 1615?), a senior member of the King's Company, played mainly character parts such as Voltore in *Volpone* and Poins in *Henry IV, Part I*.

Corey, Mrs John, née Katherine Mitchell (born *c.* 1635), one of the first English actresses and women members of the King's Company, who often played comic servants and bawds. Her roles had included Doll Common in *The Alchemist*, Lady Would-be in *Volpone*, and Mrs Joyner in *Love in a Wood*.

PROLOGUE

Spoken by Mr Hart

Poets, like cudgelled bullies, never do
At first or second blow submit to you;
But will provoke you still and ne'er have done,
Till you are weary first with laying on.
The late so baffled scribbler of this day,   5
Though he stands trembling, bids me boldly say,
What we before most plays are used to do,
For poets out of fear first draw on you;
In a fierce prologue the still pit defy,
And, ere you speak, like Castril give the lie.   10
But though our Bayeses' battles oft I've fought,
And with bruised knuckles their dear conquests bought;
Nay, never yet feared odds upon the stage,
In prologue dare not hector with the age,
But would take quarter from your saving hands,   15
Though Bayes within all yielding countermands,
Says you confederate wits no quarter give,
Therefore his play shan't ask your leave to live.
Well, let the vain rash fop, by huffing so,
Think to obtain the better terms of you;   20
But we, the actors, humbly will submit,
Now, and at any time, to a full pit;
Nay, often we anticipate your rage,

---

1 *bullies* London street ruffians
4 *laying on* inflicting blows
5 *late so baffled scribbler* Wycherley himself; either because *The Gentleman Dancing-Master*
   (1672) had not succeeded on the stage, or because *The Plain Dealer*, which may have
   already been written, had not yet been staged
10 *Castril* the 'angry boy' in Jonson's *The Alchemist*, who accuses Subtle of lying almost
   before he speaks (IV.ii.19)
11 *our Bayeses' battles* our poets' battles generally, though the speaker had played heroic
   parts in Dryden's tragedies, and the name Bayes was associated especially with Dryden.
   See 1.16 below.
14 *hector with the age* attack contemporary taste
16 *Bayes within* Wycherley behind the scenes
17 *confederate* conspiring (to damn the play)
19 *huffing* blustering

And murder poets for you on our stage.
We set no guards upon our tiring-room, 25
But when with flying colours there you come,
We patiently, you see, give up to you
Our poets, virgins, nay, our matrons too.

25 *tiring-room* dressing room
27–8 See II.i.360–2 and note.

The Country Wife

Act I, Scene i

Enter HORNER, *and* QUACK *following him at a distance*

HORNER (*Aside*)
A quack is as fit for a pimp as a midwife for a bawd; they are still
but in their way both helpers of nature. – Well, my dear doctor,
hast thou done what I desired?

QUACK
I have undone you for ever with the women, and reported you
throughout the whole town as bad as an <u>eunuch</u>, with as much   5
trouble as if I had made you one in earnest.

HORNER
But have you told all the midwives you know, the orange wenches
at the playhouses, the city husbands, and old fumbling keepers of
this end of the town? For they'll be the readiest to report it.

QUACK
I have told all the chamber-maids, waiting-women, tire-women   10
and old women of my acquaintance; nay, and whispered it as a
secret to 'em, and to the whisperers of Whitehall. So that you need
not doubt 'twill spread, and you will be as odious to the handsome
young women as –

HORNER
As the smallpox. Well –   15

QUACK
And to the married women of this end of the town as –

1   *still* always
7   *orange wenches* sellers of oranges and other refreshments
8   *city husbands* men who will be glad to hear of Horner's impotence and, according to a
    convention of Restoration comedy, easily cuckolded. There was hostility between citi-
    zens and courtiers, the citizens accusing the courtiers of immorality, and the courtiers
    accusing the citizens of hypocrisy.
8–9 *old fumbling keepers of this end of the town* incompetent keepers of mistresses living in
    the fashionable part of the town. From I.i.262–75 we gather that Horner lives in Russell
    Street, Covent Garden.
10 *tire-women* ladies' maids, or dressmakers
12 *Whitehall* the public rooms at the King's palace, where gossip flourished

[39]

HORNER

As the great ones; nay, as their own husbands.

QUACK

And to the city dames as Aniseed Robin of filthy and contemptible
memory; and they will frighten their children with your name,
especially their females.   20

HORNER

And cry, 'Horner's coming to carry you away!' I am only afraid 'twill
not be believed. You told 'em 'twas by an English-French disaster,
and an English-French surgeon, who has given me at once not only
a cure but an antidote for the future against that damned malady,
and that worse distemper, love, and all other women's evils?   25

QUACK

Your late journey into France has made it the more credible, and
your being here a fortnight before you appeared in public looks
as if you apprehended the shame; which I wonder you do not.
Well, I have been hired by young gallants to belie 'em t'other way,
but you are the first would be thought a man unfit for women.   30

HORNER

Dear Master Doctor, let vain rogues be contented only to be
thought abler men than they are, generally 'tis all the pleasure they
have; but mine lies another way.

QUACK

You take, methinks, a very preposterous way to it, and as ridiculous as if we operators in physic should put forth bills to disparage 35
our medicaments, with hopes to gain customers.

HORNER

Doctor, there are quacks in love, as well as physic, who get but the
fewer and worse patients for their boasting. A good name is

17   *the great ones* syphilis; the great pox, or syphilis, as opposed to the small ones, or small-
     pox. Pox is the plural of pock.
18   *Aniseed Robin* well-known hermaphrodite who sold aniseed water (a carminative) on
     the London streets; said to have been both a father and a mother (Charles Cotton, *Poems*,
     ed. John Beresford, p. 288)
22–23 *English-French disaster, and an English-French surgeon* Could mean pox, caught with the
     aid of an English bawd, and operated on by a surgeon specialising in venereal disease;
     everything to do with pox could be loosely associated with France. This interpretation
     is supported by Horner's remark at V.iv.55. But as I.i. emphasises that Horner has been
     in France, Lady Fidget thinks the disaster and/or operation has taken place there; see
     II.i.561–2.
23–24 *not only a cure but an antidote* because the story is that the surgeon has made him a
     eunuch

seldom got by giving it oneself, and women no more than honour
are compassed by bragging. Come, come, doctor, the wisest lawyer   40
never discovers the merits of his cause till the trial. The wealthiest
man conceals his riches, and the cunning gamester his play. Shy
husbands and keepers, like old rooks, are not to be cheated but by
a new unpractised trick. False friendship will pass now no more
than false dice upon 'em; no, not in the city.   45

Enter BOY

BOY
There are two ladies and a gentleman coming up.   [*Exit* BOY]

HORNER
A pox! Some unbelieving sisters of my former acquaintance who,
I am afraid, expect their sense should be satisfied of the falsity of
the report.

Enter SIR JASPAR, LADY FIDGET *and Mrs* DAINTY FIDGET

No; this formal fool and women!   50
QUACK
His wife and sister.
SIR JASPAR
My coach breaking just now before your door sir, I look upon as
an occasional reprimand to me sir, for not kissing your hands sir,
since your coming out of France sir; and so my disaster sir, has
been my good fortune sir; and this is my wife, and sister sir.   55
HORNER
What then, sir?

40 *compassed* won
41 *discovers* reveals
43 *rooks* tricksters. See also I.i. 229–30.
44–5 *pass upon* impose upon; *not in the city* not even among the citizens
47 *sisters* disguised prostitutes (Farmer and Henley)
50 *formal* ceremonious
52–70 Horner mocks Sir Jaspar's repetition of 'sir'. I have followed Q1 in omitting commas
before 'sir' in Sir Jaspar's speeches at ll. 52–5 and 61, and in inserting them before it in
Horner's speeches; as Peter Malekin says, Q1 hints at how the scene was or should be
played ('Wycherley's Dramatic Skills and the Interpretation of *The Country Wife*', *Durham
University Journal*, vol. 61 (1969), 32–40). But elsewhere the omission of commas before
'sir' does not seem significant, and I have followed modern practice in inserting them.
53 *occasional* timely

SIR JASPAR

My lady, and sister, sir. – Wife, this is Master Horner.

LADY FIDGET

Master Horner, husband!

SIR JASPAR

My lady, my Lady Fidget, sir.

HORNER

So, sir.   60

SIR JASPAR

Won't you be acquainted with her sir? (*Aside*) So, the report is true, I find, by his coldness or aversion to the sex; but I'll play the wag with him. – Pray salute my wife, my lady, sir.

[margin handwriting: Test of the nouns are one]

HORNER

I will kiss no man's wife, sir, for him, sir; I have taken my eternal leave, sir, of the sex already, sir.   65

SIR JASPAR (*Aside*)

Ha, ha, ha! I'll plague him yet. – Not know my wife, sir?

HORNER

I do know your wife, sir, she's a woman, sir, and consequently a monster, sir, a greater monster than a husband, sir.

SIR JASPAR

A husband! How, sir?

HORNER (*Makes horns*)

So, sir. But I make no more cuckolds, sir.   70

SIR JASPAR

Ha, ha, ha! Mercury, Mercury!

LADY FIDGET

Pray, Sir Jaspar, let us be gone from this rude fellow.

DAINTY

Who, by his breeding, would think he had ever been in France?

LADY FIDGET

Foh! he's but too much a French fellow, such as hate women of

---

62–3 *play the wag with him* have a joke at his expense. See also IV.iii. 148–51.

70 sd *horns* sign of a cuckold, made by holding the fists at the temples, and extending the index fingers; *cuckolds* husbands of adulterous wives. For obvious reasons adulterers were known as cuckoos, and their victims came to be called cuckolds, but it is not clear why cuckolds were supposed to have horns.

71 *Mercury* god associated with wit. Also, substance used to treat venereal disease; but perhaps Horner making horns reminds Sir Jaspar of representations of Mercury with a winged hat.

74 *French fellow* fop

quality and virtue for their love to their husbands, Sir Jaspar. A   75
woman is hated by 'em as much for loving her husband as for loving their money. But pray let's be gone.

HORNER

You do well, madam, for I have nothing that you came for. I have
brought over not so much as a bawdy picture, new postures, nor
the second part of the *École des Filles*, nor –   80

QUACK (*Apart* to HORNER)

Hold for shame sir! What d'ye mean? You'll ruin yourself for ever
with the sex –

SIR JASPAR

Ha, ha, ha! He hates women perfectly, I find.

DAINTY

What pity 'tis he should.

LADY FIDGET

Ay, he's a base rude fellow for't; but affectation makes not a woman   85
more odious to them than virtue.

HORNER

Because your virtue is your greatest affectation, madam.

LADY FIDGET

How, you saucy fellow! Would you wrong my honour?

HORNER

If I could.

LADY FIDGET

How d'ye mean, sir?   90

SIR JASPAR

Ha, ha, ha! No, he can't wrong your ladyship's honour, upon my
honour! He, poor man – hark you in your ear – a mere eunuch.

LADY FIDGET

O filthy French beast! foh, foh! Why do we stay? Let's be gone. I
can't endure the sight of him.

SIR JASPAR

Stay but till the chairs come. They'll be here presently.   95

LADY FIDGET

No, no.

---

79 *postures* erotic engravings used to illustrate pornographic books
80 *École des Filles* (1668), 'the most bawdy, lewd book that ever I saw ... so that I was ashamed
    of reading it' (Pepys, Diary, 16 January 1668)
88 *How* what
95 *chairs* sedan chairs
    presently at once

SIR JASPAR

Nor can I stay longer. 'Tis – let me see – a quarter and a half quarter of a minute past eleven. The Council will be sat, I must away. Business must be preferred always before love and ceremony with the wise, Master Horner.   100

HORNER

And the impotent, Sir Jaspar.

SIR JASPAR

Ay, ay, the impotent, Master Horner, ha, ha, ha!

LADY FIDGET

What, leave us with a filthy man alone in his lodgings?

SIR JASPAR

He's an innocent man now, you know. Pray stay, I'll hasten the chairs to you. Master Horner, your servant; I should be glad to see   105
you at my house. Pray come and dine with me, and play at cards with my wife after dinner; you are fit for women at that game yet, ha, ha! (*Aside*) 'Tis as much a husband's prudence to provide innocent diversion for a wife as to hinder her unlawful pleasures; and he had better employ her, than let her employ herself. – Farewell.   110

                                                        Exit SIR JASPAR

HORNER

Your servant, Sir Jaspar.

LADY FIDGET

I will not stay with him, foh!

HORNER

Nay, madam, I beseech you stay, if it be but to see I can be as civil to ladies yet as they would desire.

LADY FIDGET

No, no, foh! You cannot be civil to ladies.   115

DAINTY

You as civil as ladies would desire?

LADY FIDGET

No, no, no! foh, foh, foh!   *Exeunt* LADY FIDGET *and* DAINTY

---

  97 *Council* Privy Council
  98 *Business* at court, not in the City. See Introduction, p.5
 110 *employ* keep busy
113–5 *civil* probably with a sexual connotation: 'You are both very civil gentlemen – and my
        wife, there, is a very civil gentlewoman; therefore I don't doubt but many civil things
        have passed between you' (Vanbrugh, *The Provoked Wife*, ed. James L. Smith, V.ii.83–5).

QUACK

Now I think, I, or you yourself rather, have done your business
with the women.

HORNER

Thou art an ass. Don't you see already, upon the report and my   120
carriage, this grave man of business leaves his wife in my lodgings,
invites me to his house and wife, who before would not be
acquainted with me out of jealousy?

QUACK

Nay, by this means you may be the more acquainted with the
husbands, but the less with the wives.   125

HORNER

Let me alone; if I can but abuse the husbands, I'll soon disabuse
the wives. Stay; I'll reckon you up the advantages I am like to have
by my stratagem. First, I shall be rid of all my old acquaintances,
the most insatiable sorts of duns, that invade our lodgings in a
morning. And next to the pleasure of making a new mistress is   130
that of being rid of an old one, and of all old debts; love, when it
comes to be so, is paid the most unwillingly.

QUACK

Well, you may be so rid of your old acquaintances, but how will
you get any new ones?

HORNER

Doctor, thou wilt never make a good chemist, thou art so   135
incredulous and impatient. Ask but all the young fellows of the
town, if they do not lose more time, like huntsmen, in starting the
game, than in running it down. One knows not where to find 'em
who will, or will not. Women of quality are so civil, you can hardly
distinguish love from good breeding, and a man is often mistaken.   140
But now I can be sure she that shows an aversion to me loves the

---

118 *done your business* ruined you
121 *carriage* conduct
126 *abuse* deceive. The word probably has modern sense at I.i.233.
129 *duns* importunate creditors; apparently referring to I.i.47–8
130 *next* Q2–5, O (next, Q1). The Q1 comma suggests Horner is counting his advantages,
   'first' one 'and next' another. But he actually says 'next to' the pleasure of taking a mistress is that of discarding one; so I have discarded the comma. Markley suggests that
   Horner, unable to count many advantages, changes his mind about what he is saying.
132 *so*, i.e. an old debt
135 *chemist* alchemist. In Jonson's *The Alchemist* the clients' incredulity and impatience are
   supposed to harm the alchemical process.
136–41 The problem is to distinguish the game from other creatures.

sport; as those women that are gone, whom I warrant to be right.
And then the next thing is, your women of honour, as you call 'em,
are only chary of their reputations, not their persons, and 'tis
scandal they would avoid, not men. Now may I have, by the   145
reputation of an eunuch, the privileges of one; and be seen in a
lady's chamber in a morning as early as her husband; kiss
virgins before their parents or lovers; and may be, in short, the
passe-partout of the town. Now doctor?

QUACK

Nay, now you shall be the doctor. And your process is so new that   150
we do not know but it may succeed.

HORNER

Not so new neither. *Probatum est*, doctor.

QUACK

Well, I wish you luck and many patients whilst I go to mine.

Exit QUACK

Enter HARCOURT *and* DORILANT *to* HORNER

HARCOURT

Come, your appearance at the play yesterday has, I hope, hard-
ened you for the future against the women's contempt and the   155
men's raillery, and now you'll abroad , as you were wont.

HORNER   *mocking*

Did I not bear it bravely?

DORILANT

With a most theatrical impudence! Nay, more than the
orange-wenches show there, or a drunken vizard-mask, or
a great-bellied actress. Nay, or the most impudent of   160
creatures, an ill poet. Or, what is yet more impudent, a second-
hand critic.

HORNER

But what say the ladies? Have they no pity?

---

142 *right* ready for the sport, 'game'. See *The Gentleman Dancing-Master* III.i.530, and the
note in Friedman, p. 189.
149 *passe-partout* person having leave to go anywhere
150 *doctor* alchemist; *process* alchemical experiment
152 *probatum est* proved or tested; phrase written on prescriptions. Horner apparently means
that in the sex game nothing is wholly new. Wycherley possibly hints at his own bor-
rowing from Terence; see Introduction, p.17.
159 *vizard-mask* (here) prostitute. Just after the Restoration masks had been fashionable
wear, but by this time they had become professional gear.

the pox? prostituted?

HARCOURT

What ladies? The vizard-masks, you know, never pity a man when
all's gone, though in their service.   165

DORILANT

And for the women in the boxes, you'd never pity them when 'twas
in your power.

HARCOURT

They say 'tis pity, but all that deal with common women should
be served so.

DORILANT

Nay, I dare swear, they won't admit you to play at cards with   170
them, go to plays with 'em, or do the little duties which other
shadows of men are wont to do for 'em.

HORNER

Who do you call shadows of men?

keeping up the pretence

DORILANT

Half-men.

HORNER

What, boys?   *TEASING*   175

DORILANT

Ay, your old boys, old *beaux garçons*, who like superannuated
stallions are suffered to run, feed, and whinny with the
mares as long as they live, though they can do nothing else.

HORNER

Well, a pox on love and wenching! Women serve but to keep a
man from better company. Though I can't enjoy them, I   180
shall you the more. Good fellowship and friendship are lasting,
rational, and manly pleasures.

HARCOURT

For all that, give me some of those pleasures you call effeminate
too. They help to relish one another.

HORNER

They disturb one another.   185

---

165 *all* sexual potency or money
166 *women in the boxes* 'persons of the best quality, among whom are generally very few men'
     occupied the boxes. See Introduction, p. 20.
176 *beaux garçons* fops

[47]

HARCOURT

No, mistresses are like books; if you pore upon them too much
they doze you and make you unfit for company, but if used
discreetly you are the fitter for conversation by 'em.

DORILANT

A mistress should be like a little country retreat near the town; not
to dwell in constantly, but only for a night and away, to taste the
town the better when a man returns. 190

HORNER

I tell you, 'tis as hard to be a good fellow, a good friend, and a lover
of women, as 'tis to be a good fellow, a good friend, and a lover of
money. You cannot follow both, then choose your side: wine gives
you liberty, love takes it away. 195

DORILANT

Gad, he's in the right on't.

HORNER

Wine gives you joy; love, grief and tortures, besides the surgeon's.
Wine makes us witty; love, only sots. Wine makes us sleep; love
breaks it.

DORILANT

By the world, he has reason, Harcourt. 200

HORNER

Wine makes –

DORILANT

Ay wine makes us – makes us princes; love makes us beggars, poor
rogues, i'gad – and wine –

DORILANT

So there's one converted. No, no, love and wine, oil and vinegar.

HARCOURT

I grant it; love will still be uppermost. 205

---

187 *doze* make drowsy or dull

188 *conversation* intercourse; *double entendre*. See also II.i.560 and III.ii.20.

189 *country* sexual; having a cunt; common *double entendres*. See Partridge; and Marie Collins,
'Hamlet and the Lady's Lap', *Notes and Queries*, vol. 28 (1981), 130–2.

197 *tortures, besides the surgeon's. Wine* ed. (tortures; besides the Chirurgeon's Wine
Q1–5, O). The emended punctuation is supported by Wycherley's *Plays* (1720 and 1731
editions). Markley suggests that *besides the surgeon's* is an afterthought suggested by Dorilant and Harcourt's laughter.

200 *he has reason* This translates *il a raison*, he is right. Perhaps Dorilant, as his name suggests, is French or frenchified. In Dryden's *Sir Martin Mar-all*, Moody, a lover of 'the true
old English manliness', considers 'you have reason' a deplorable 'town phrase' (III.i.62).

HORNER

Come, for my part I will have only those glorious, manly pleasures of being very drunk and very slovenly.

Enter BOY

BOY

Master Sparkish is below, sir.   [*Exit* BOY]

HARCOURT

What, my dear friend! A rogue that is fond of me, only I think for abusing him.   210

DORILANT

No, he can no more think the men laugh at him than that women jilt him, his opinion of himself is so good.

HORNER

Well, there's another pleasure by drinking I thought not of; I shall lose his acquaintance, because he cannot drink. And you know 'tis a very hard thing to be rid of him, for he's one of those nauseous   215
offerers at wit, who, like the worst fiddlers, run themselves into all companies.

HARCOURT

One that by being in the company of men of sense would pass for one.

HORNER

And may so to the short-sighted world, as a false jewel amongst   220
true ones is not discerned at a distance. His company is as troublesome to us as a cuckold's when you have a mind to his wife's.

HARCOURT

No, the rogue will not let us enjoy one another, but ravishes our conversation, though he signifies no more to't than Sir Martin Mar-all's gaping and awkward thrumming upon the lute does to   225
his man's voice and music.

---

210 *abusing* See I.i. 126.
214 *he cannot drink* like Dapperwit, the would-be wit in *Love in a Wood*. Vincent tries to make him drink because 'there is no other way to silence him' (I.ii. 16–17).
220 *short-sighted* Q2–5, O (short-sighed Q1)
224–5 *Sir Martin Mar-all* hero of Dryden's *The Feigned Innocence; or, Sir Martin Mar-all* (1667), who serenades his mistress in mime while his hidden servant sings and plays the lute. As usual Sir Martin mars all by continuing after his servant has finished.

[49]

DORILANT

And to pass for a wit in town shows himself a fool every night to us, that are guilty of the plot.

HORNER

Such wits as he are, to a company of reasonable men, like rooks to the gamesters, who only fill a room at the table, but are so far from contributing to the play that they only serve to spoil the fancy of those that do. 230

DORILANT

Nay, they are used like rooks too, snubbed, checked, and abused; yet the rogues will hang on.

HORNER

A pox on 'em, and all that force nature, and would be still what she forbids 'em! Affectation is her greatest monster. 235

HARCOURT

Most men are the contraries to that they would seem. Your bully, you see, is a coward with a long sword; the little, humbly fawning physician with his ebony cane is he that destroys men.

DORILANT

The usurer, a poor rogue possessed of mouldy bonds and mortgages; and we they call spendthrifts are only wealthy, who lay out his money upon daily new purchases of pleasure. 240

HORNER

Ay, your arrantest cheat is your trustee or executor; your jealous man, the greatest cuckold; your churchman, the greatest atheist; and your noisy, pert rogue of a wit, the greatest fop, dullest ass, and worst company; as you shall see, for here he comes. 245

Enter SPARKISH *to them*

SPARKISH

How is't, sparks, how is't? Well, faith, Harry, I must rally thee a

---

228 *us, that are guilty of the plot* those of us who have conspired to encourage him
229 *rooks* victims of tricksters. See also I.i.52.
230 *room* place
232 *fancy* pleasure
233 *checked* taunted
235 *would be still* persist in trying to be
239 *ebony cane* usually carried by physicians at the time
241 *are only* are the only ones who are
243–4 *your jealous man, the greatest cuckold* explained by Horner at III.ii.58–61
247 *sparks* young men about town; usually depreciatory. See note on Sparkish, p.4.
       rally make fun of; a fashionable word. See II.i. 155 and note.

little, ha, ha, ha! upon the report in town of thee, ha, ha, ha! I can't
hold i'faith! Shall I speak?

HORNER

Yes, but you'll be so bitter then.   250

SPARKISH

Honest Dick and Frank here shall answer for me, I will not be
extreme bitter, by the universe.

HARCOURT

We will be bound in ten thousand pound bond, he shall not be
bitter at all.

DORILANT

Nor sharp, nor sweet.   255

HORNER

What, not downright insipid?

SPARKISH

Nay then, since you are so brisk and provoke me, take what
follows. You must know, I was discoursing and rallying with some
ladies yesterday, and they happened to talk of the fine new
signs in town.   260

HORNER

Very fine ladies, I believe.

SPARKISH

Said I, 'I know where the best new sign is'. 'Where?' says one of the
ladies. 'In Covent Garden', I replied. Said another, 'In what street?'
'In Russell Street', answered I. 'Lord', says another, 'I'm sure there
was ne'er a fine new sign there yesterday'. 'Yes, but there was', said   265
I again, 'and it came out of France, and has been there a fortnight'.

DORILANT

A pox! I can hear no more, prithee.

252 *extreme* extremely

257 *brisk* smart; depreciatory. In Etherege's *The Man of Mode* (1676) Sir Fopling Flutter is
'the gay, the giddy, brisk, insipid, noisy fool' (V.i. 95–6); in *Pilgrim's Progress* (1678) Ignorance is 'a very brisk lad' from 'the country of Conceit'.

260 *signs* tradesmen's signs or symbols. See III.ii. 202.

263 *Covent Garden* then a fashionable part of London, with some well-known taverns and
coffee houses

264 *Rusell Street* off the east side of Covent Garden

266 *again* in reply

HORNER

No, hear him out; let him tune his crowd a while.

HARCOURT

The worst music, the greatest preparation.

SPARKISH

Nay, faith, I'll make you laugh. 'It cannot be', says a third lady. 'Yes,   270
yes', quoth I again. Says a fourth lady –

HORNER

Look to't, we'll have no more ladies.

SPARKISH

No – then mark, mark, now. Said I to the fourth, 'Did you never
see Master Horner? He lodges in Russell Street, and he's a sign of
a man, you know, since he came out of France!' He, ha, he!   275

HORNER

But the devil take me, if thine be the sign of a jest.

SPARKISH

With that they all fell a-laughing, till they bepissed themselves.
What, but it does not move you, methinks? Well, I see one had as
good go to law without a witness, as break a jest without a laugher
on one's side. Come, come sparks, but where do we dine? I have   280
left at Whitehall an earl, to dine with you.

DORILANT

Why, I thought thou hadst loved a man with a title better than a
suit with a French trimming to't.

HARCOURT

Go to him again.

SPARKISH

No, sir, a wit to me is the greatest title in the world.   285

HORNER

But go dine with your earl, sir; he may be exceptious. We are your
friends, and will not take it ill to be left, I do assure you.

---

268 *crowd* fiddle; perhaps a quibble on the more familiar sense, as Sparkish seems to know
     a lot of ladies

274 *sign* mere semblance

278 *I* Q3, O (*omitted*, Q1–2, 4–5)

278–9 i.e., a joke needs someone to laugh at it, as a lawsuit needs a witness

283 *suit with a French trimming* fashionable suit; unlikely to refer also to Horner's supposed
     impotence, as Dorilant is supporting him against Sparkish

284 *Go to him again* Q2–5, O (Go, to him again Q1). Holland defends Q1 as meaning Har-
     court urges Dorilant to tease Sparkish further; but if so Dorilant ignores him, and
     Harcourt again urges Sparkish to return to the Earl in his next speech.

286 *exceptious* peevish

[52]

HARCOURT
  Nay, faith, he shall go to him.

SPARKISH
  Nay, pray, gentlemen.

DORILANT
  We'll thrust you out, if you won't. What, disappoint anybody   290
  for us?

SPARKISH
  Nay, dear gentlemen, hear me.

HORNER
  No, no sir, by no means; pray go, sir.

SPARKISH
  Why, dear rogues –

DORILANT
  No, no.   *They all thrust him out of the room*   295

ALL
  Ha, ha, ha!

                    SPARKISH *returns*

SPARKISH
  But, sparks, pray hear me. What, d'ye think I'll eat, then, with gay
  shallow fops and silent coxcombs? I think wit as necessary at
  dinner as a glass of good wine, and that's the reason I never have
  any stomach when I eat alone. Come, but where do we dine?   300

HORNER
  Even where you will.

SPARKISH
  At Chateline's?

DORILANT
  Yes, if you will.

SPARKISH
  Or at the Cock?

DORILANT
  Yes, if you please.   305

SPARKISH
  Or at the Dog and Partridge?

---

  300 *stomach* appetite
  302 *Chateline's* French restaurant in Covent Garden
  304 *the Cock* probably the tavern in Bow Street, Covent Garden. Wycherley went there, and
       set *The Plain Dealer* V.ii there.
  306 *the Dog and Partridge* tavern in Fleet Street; probably the least acceptable of Sparkish's
       suggestions

HORNER

Ay, if you have a mind to't, for we shall dine at neither.

SPARKISH

Pshaw! with your fooling we shall lose the new play. And I would
no more miss seeing a new play the first day than I would miss
sitting in the wits' row. Therefore I'll go fetch my mistress   310
and away.   *Exit* SPARKISH

Manent HORNER, HARCOURT, DORILANT. *Enter to them*
PINCHWIFE

HORNER

Who have we here? Pinchwife!

PINCHWIFE

Gentlemen, your humble servant.

HORNER

Well, Jack, by thy long absence from the town, the grumness of thy
countenance, and the slovenliness of thy habit, I should give thee   315
joy, should I not, of marriage?

PINCHWIFE (*Aside*)

Death! does he know I'm married too? I thought to have concealed
it from him at least. – My long stay in the country will excuse my
dress, and I have a suit of law, that brings me up to town, that puts
me out of humour. Besides, I must give Sparkish tomorrow   320
five thousand pound to lie with my sister.

HORNER

Nay, you country gentlemen, rather than not purchase, will buy
anything; and he is a cracked title, if we may quibble. Well, but
am I to give thee joy? I heard thou wert married.

PINCHWIFE

What then?   325

---

307   *a mind* Q2–5, O (mind Q1)
      neither none of them (*OED* B. 2.c)
310   *sitting* Q3 (setting Q1–2, 4–5, O)
      the wits' row with other wits, in the pit
311   sd *manent* remain
314   *grumness* moroseness. Don Diego, in *The Gentleman Dancing Master*, boasts of being
      'grum, and jealous' (II.i.36).
321   *five thousand pound* as a dowry. Pinchwife must be wealthy.
322   *purchase* acquire land or property by purchase
323   *cracked title* a property in a poor state of repair, or bankrupt, or (as applied to Sparkish)
      'cracked'. He is a bad buy.

HORNER

Why, the next thing that is to be heard is, thou'rt a cuckold.

PINCHWIFE (*Aside*)

Insupportable name!

HORNER

But I did not expect marriage from such a whoremaster as you,
one that knew the town so much, and women so well.

PINCHWIFE

Why, I have married no London wife.   330

HORNER

Pshaw! that's all one. That grave circumspection in marrying a
country wife is like refusing a deceitful, pampered Smithfield jade,
to go and be cheated by a friend in the country.

PINCHWIFE (*Aside*)

A pox on him and his simile! – At least we are a little surer
of the breed there, know what her keeping has been, whether   335
foiled or unsound.

HORNER

Come, come, I have known a clap gotten in Wales. And there are
cozens, justices, clerks, and chaplains in the country; I won't say
coachmen! But she's handsome and young?

328 *whoremaster* experienced lecher
329 *one that knew the town so much* Horner ridicules Pinchwife's claim before he has even
made it; see ll.383–4, 404. Later, Dorilant ridicules it too; see ll. 420.
332 *Smithfield* horse market with reputation for sharp practice: 'This town two bargains has,
not worth one farthing, / A Smithfield horse, and a wife of Covent-Garden' (Dryden,
The Kind Keeper (1680), Epilogue).
jade both worn-out horse and disreputable woman
335 *keeping* how she has been kept; *double entendre.* See I.i.405 and note.
336 *foiled* both injured (horse) and deflowered (woman)
unsound diseased
337 *clap* gonorrhoea
Wales to Londoners a remote part of the country
338 *cozens* cozeners, cheaters; needlessly altered to 'cousins' by some editors. Horner has mentioned cheating at l. 333.
justices, clerks, Q1 (justices clerks, Q2–5, O). Q1 adds one to Homer's list of supposedly
respectable people who spread venereal disease.
339 *coachmen* legendary studs. Dapperwit regards Lady Flippant's coachman as his rival (*Love
in a Wood* I.ii. 232–3); Mrs Caution is accused of having fancied her father's coachman
(*The Gentleman Dancing-Master* I.i. 319).

PINCHWIFE (*Aside*)

    I'll answer as I should do. – No, no, she has no beauty but her   340
    youth; no attraction but her modesty; wholesome, homely, and
    housewifely, that's all.

DORILANT

    He talks as like a grazier as he looks.

PINCHWIFE

    She's too awkward, ill-favoured, and silly to bring to town.

HORNER

    Then methinks you should bring her, to be taught breeding.   345

PINCHWIFE

    To be taught! No, sir, I thank you. Good wives and private soldiers
    should be ignorant. [*Aside*] I'll keep her from your instructions, I
    warrant you.

HARCOURT (*Aside*)

    The rogue is as jealous as if his wife were not ignorant.

HORNER

    Why, if she be ill-favoured, there will be less danger here for you   350
    than by leaving her in the country. We have such variety of
    dainties that we are seldom hungry.

DORILANT

    But they have always coarse, constant, swingeing stomachs in the
    country.

HARCOURT

    Foul feeders indeed.   355

DORILANT

    And your hospitality is great there.

HARCOURT

    Open house, every man's welcome!

PINCHWIFE

    So, so, gentlemen.

---

340 *as I should do* perhaps 'as you would expect; we expect lies. This was altered in Lee's *The
     Country Wife* to 'I'll answer him accordingly' and cut in Garrick's *The Country Girl.*

343 *grazier* one who fattens cattle for the market

344 *silly* ignorant

345 sp. HORNER (Har. Q1–5, O). But the Q1 reading could be a printer's error for Hor., i.e.,
     Horner; Pinchwife's next aside refers to Horner rather than Harcourt.
     breeding gentility and, probably, pregnancy

349 sd (*Aside*) Q1–5, O. But the line need not be spoken aside, so perhaps the sd is meant for
     Pinchwife's aside at ll. 401–2

353 *swingeing stomachs* huge appetites

HORNER

But, prithee, why would'st thou marry her? If she be ugly, ill-bred, and silly, she must be rich then? 360

PINCHWIFE

As rich as if she brought me twenty thousand pound out of this town; for she'll be as sure not to spend her moderate portion as a London baggage would be to spend hers, let it be what it would; so 'tis all one. Then, because she's ugly, she's the likelier to be my own; and being ill-bred, she'll 365 hate conversation; and since silly and innocent, will not know the difference betwixt a man of one-and-twenty and one of forty.

HORNER

Nine – to my knowledge; but if she be silly, she'll expect as much from a man of forty-nine as from him of one-and-twenty. 370 But methinks wit is more necessary than beauty; and I think no young woman ugly that has it, and no handsome woman agreeable without it.

PINCHWIFE

'Tis my maxim, he's a fool that marries, but he's a greater that does not marry a fool. What is wit in a wife good for, but to make 375 a man a cuckold?

HORNER

Yes, to keep it from his knowledge.

PINCHWIFE

A fool cannot contrive to make her husband a cuckold.

HORNER

No, but she'll club with a man that can; and what is worse, if she cannot make her husband a cuckold, she'll make him jealous, and 380 pass for one, and then 'tis all one.

PINCHWIFE

Well, well, I'll take care for one, my wife shall make me no cuckold, though she had your help, Master Horner; I understand the town, sir.

DORILANT (*Aside*)

His help! 385

HARCOURT (*Aside*)

He's come newly to town, it seems, and has not heard how things are with him.

364 *'tis all one* it's as if she had brought me a fortune
379 *club* get together

HORNER

But tell me, has marriage cured thee of whoring, which it seldom does?

HARCOURT

'Tis more than age can do. 390

HORNER

No, the word is, I'll marry and live honest. But a marriage vow is like a penitent gamester's oath, and entering into bonds and penalties to stint himself to such a particular small sum at play for the future, which makes him but the more eager, and not being able to hold out, loses his money again, and his 395 forfeit to boot.

DORLIANT

Ay, ay, a gamester will be a gamester whilst his money lasts, and a whoremaster, whilst his vigour.

HARCOURT

Nay, I have known 'em, when they are broke and can lose no more, keep a-fumbling with the box in their hands to fool with only, and 400 hinder other gamesters.

DORILANT

That had wherewithal to make lusty stakes.

PINCHWIFE

Well, gentlemen, you may laugh at me, but you shall never lie with my wife; I know the town.

HORNER

But prithee, was not the way you were in better? Is not keeping 405 better than marriage?

---

391 *word* usual saying
honest chaste
393 *such* such and such
play gambling
395 *hold out* keep to his plan;
forfeit payment under the 'bonds and penalties'
399 *broke* impecunious and impotent (Dixon)
400 *box* both receptacle for dice and vagina; noted in *Modern Language Review*, vol. 82 (1987), 31 by Ian Donaldson, who draws attention to the source in Horace, *Satires* 2.7. 15–18, and to similar ideas in Rochester, 'The Disabled Debauchee' (*c.* 1675)
402 *lusty stakes* big bets and, probably, erections. Some such *double entendre* is needed to complete the analogy between a gambler and a lecher, and to explain the wits' laughter.
405 *keeping* supporting a mistress. See also I.i. 335.

PINCHWIFE

A pox on't! The jades would jilt me; I could never keep a whore to myself.

HORNER

So, then, you only married to keep a whore to yourself. Well, but let me tell you, women, as you say, are like soldiers, made constant   410 and loyal by good pay rather than by oaths and covenants. Therefore I'd advise my friends to keep rather than marry, since too I find, by your example, it does not serve one's turn; for I saw you yesterday in the eighteen-penny place with a pretty country wench!

PINCHWIFE (*Aside*)

How the devil! Did he see my wife then? I sat there that she might   415 not be seen. But she shall never go to a play again.

HORNER

What, dost them blush at nine-and-forty for having been seen with a wench?

DORILANT

No, faith, I warrant 'twas his wife, which he seated there out of sight, for he's a cunning rogue, and understands the town.   420

HARCOURT

He blushes! Then 'twas his wife; for men are now more ashamed to be seen with them in public than with a wench.

PINCHWIFE (*Aside*)

Hell and damnation! I'm undone, since Horner has seen her, and they know 'twas she.

HORNER

But prithee, was it thy wife? She was exceedingly pretty; I was in   425 love with her at that distance.

PINCHWIFE

You are like never to be nearer to her. Your servant, gentlemen.

Offers to go

HORNER

Nay, prithee stay.

PINCHWIFE

I cannot, I will not.

---

414 *eighteen-penny place* the middle gallery in the theatre, the best place for a man to stop his wife being seen by the gallants in the pit and the boxes. But it was also frequented by prostitutes.
sd *offers* attempts

HORNER

Come, you shall dine with us.   430

PINCHWIFE

I have dined already.

HORNER

Come, I know thou hast not. I'll treat thee, dear rogue. Thou shan't
spend none of thy Hampshire money today.

PINCHWIFE (*Aside*)

Treat me! So, he uses me already like his cuckold!

HORNER

Nay, you shall not go.   435

PINCHWIFE

I must, I have business at home.   *Exit* PINCHWIFE

HARCOURT

To beat his wife! He's as jealous of her as a Cheapside husband
of a Covent Garden wife.

HORNER

Why, 'tis as hard to find an old whoremaster without jealousy and
the gout, as a young one without fear or the pox.   440

　　As gout in age from pox in youth proceeds,

　　So wenching past, then jealousy succeeds;

　　The worst disease that love and wenching breeds.

                                                    [*Exeunt*]

Act II, Scene i

MRS MARGERY PINCHWIFE *and* ALITHEA; PINCHWIFE
peeping behind at the door

MRS PINCHWIFE

Pray, sister, where are the best fields and woods to walk in, in
London?

432　*rogue* term of endearment as well as abuse
433　*Hampshire* the country (antonomasia), or Horner may know Pinchwife now lives there.
　　See II.i. 118.
434　See IV.iii. 269–70.
437　*Cheapside husband* bourgeois husband
438　*Covent Garden wife* upper class wife, or bourgeois wife who pretends to be upper class.
　　For Dryden's opinion of such wives, see I.i. 332 note.

ALITHEA

A pretty question! Why, sister, Mulberry Garden and St
James's Park; and for close walks, the New Exchange.

MRS PINCHWIFE

Pray, sister, tell me why my husband looks so gram here   5
in town, and keeps me up so close, and will not let me go
a-walking, nor let me wear my best gown yesterday?

ALITHEA

Oh, he's jealous, sister.

MRS PINCHWIFE

Jealous? What's that?

ALITHEA

He's afraid you should love another man.   10

MRS PINCHWIFE

How should he be afraid of my loving another man, when he will
not let me see any but himself?

ALITHEA

Did he not carry you yesterday to a play?

MRS PINCHWIFE

Ay, but we sat amongst ugly people. He would not let me
come near the gentry, who sat under us, so that I could not   15
see 'em. He told me none but naughty women sat there,
whom they toused and moused. But I would have ventured for
all that.

ALITHEA

But how did you like the play?

MRS PINCHWIFE

Indeed I was a-weary of the play, but I liked hugeously the   20
actors! They are the goodliest, properest men, sister.

3–4 *Mulberry Garden and St James's Park* fashionable meeting places; settings for scenes in
      Love in a Wood. The garden was in the park, where Buckingham Palace now stands.
   4 *close* covered
      New Exchange arcade with fasionable shops; setting for III.ii
   5 *grum* morose. He makes the same impression on Horner, I.i.314.
   6 *up so close* so closely confined
  13 *carry* take
  17 *toused and moused* tousled and mousled, engaged in sexual harrassment (*OED* mouse
      v. 3.b; Farmer and Henley, tousle)
  20 *hugeously* 'terrifically'; vulgarism
  21 *properest* most handsome

ALITHEA

Oh, but you must not like the actors, sister.

MRS PINCHWIFE

Ay, how should I help it, sister? Pray, sister, when my
husband comes in, will you ask leave for me to go a-
walking?   25

ALITHEA (*Aside*)

A-walking! Ha, ha! Lord, a country gentlewoman's leisure
is the drudgery of a foot-post; and she requires as much airing as
her husband's horses.

Enter PINCHWIFE *to them*

But here comes your husband; I'll ask, though I'm sure he'll
not grant it.   30

MRS PINCHWIFE

He says he won't let me go abroad for fear of catching the
pox.

ALITHEA

Fie, the smallpox you should say.

MRS PINCHWIFE

Oh my dear, dear bud, welcome home! Why dost thou look
so froppish? Who has nangered thee?   35

PINCHWIFE

You're a fool!   MRS PINCHWIFE *goes aside and cries*

ALITHEA

Faith, so she is, for crying for no fault, poor tender
creature!

PINCHWIFE

What, you would have her as impudent as yourself, as
arrant a jill-flirt, a gadder, a magpie, and – to say all – a mere   40
notorious town-woman?

---

27 *foot-post* messenger on foot
34 *bud* term of endearment usually applied to children. But in Garrick's. *The Country
    Girl* Lucy says 'Bud means husband . . . and if he was my husband I'd bud him, a
    surly, unreasonable beast' (II.ii). Perhaps Wycherley alludes to the cuckold's budding
    horns.
35 *froppish* fretful; *nangered* angered. Again she talks to him as if he were a child.
40 *jill-flirt* wanton girl
    gadder gadabout
    magpie chatterer

ALITHEA

Brother, you are my only censurer; and the honour of your
family shall sooner suffer in your wife there than in me, though
I take the innocent liberty of the town.

PINCHWIFE

Hark you, mistress, do not talk so before my wife. The   45
innocent liberty of the town!

ALITHEA

Why, pray, who boasts of any intrigue with me? What lampoon
has made my name notorious? What ill women frequent my
lodgings? I keep no company with any women of scandalous
reputations.   50

PINCHWIFE

No, you keep the men of scandalous reputations
company.

AUTHEA

Where? Would you not have me civil? Answer 'em in a
box at the plays, in the drawing room at Whitehall, in St James's
Park, Mulberry Garden, or –   55

PINCHWIFE

Hold, hold! Do not teach my wife where the men are
to be found! I believe she's the worse for your town
documents already. I bid you keep her in ignorance, as I
do.

MRS PINCHWIFE

Indeed, be not angry with her, bud. She will tell me   60
nothing of the town though I ask her a thousand times a
day.

PINCHWIFE

Then you are very inquisitive to know, I find!

MRS PINCHWIFE

Not I, indeed, dear. I hate London. Our placehouse in
the country is worth a thousand of't. Would I were there   65
again!

---

47 *lampoon* scurrilous satire circulating in manuscript
57–8 *town documents* lessons about the town
64 *placehouse* chief house on an estate. Suggests a wealthy background.

PINCHWIFE

So you shall, I warrant. But were you not talking of plays and players when I came in? [*To* ALITHEA] You are her encourager in such discourses.

MRS PINCHWIFE

No, indeed, dear; she chid me just now for liking the   70
player-men.

PINCHWIFE (*Aside*)

Nay, if she be so innocent as to own to me her liking them, there is no hurt in't. – Come, my poor rogue, but thou lik'st none better than me?

MRS PINCHWIFE

Yes, indeed, but I do; the player-men are finer folks.   75

PINCHWIFE

But you love none better than me?

MRS PINCHWIFE

You are mine own dear bud, and I know you; I hate a stranger.

PINCHWIFE

Ay, my dear, you must love me only, and not be like the naughty town-women, who only hate their husbands   80
and love every man else; love plays, visits, fine coaches, fine clothes, fiddles, balls, treats, and so lead a wicked town-life.

MRS PINCHWIFE

Nay, if to enjoy all these things be a town-life, London is not so bad a place, dear.   85

PINCHWIFE

How! If you love me, you must hate London.

ALITHEA [*Aside*]

The fool has forbid me discovering to her the pleasures of the town, and he is now setting her agog upon them himself.

---

71 *player-men* actors, as she called them at II.i. 21; perhaps childish language, for Pinchwife's benefit
82 *fiddles* fiddlers
    balls social gatherings
    treats entertainments
88 *setting her agog upon* making her eager for

MRS PINCHWIFE

But, husband, do the town-women love the player-men   90
too?

PINCHWIFE

Yes, I warrant you.

MRS PINCHWIFE

Ay, I warrant you.

PINCHWIFE

Why, you do not, I hope?

MRS PINCHWIFE

No, no, bud; but why have we no player-men in the   95
country?

PINCHWIFE

Ha! – Mistress Minx, ask me no more to go to a play.

MRS PINCHWIFE

Nay, why love? I did not care for going, but when you forbid
me, you make me, as't were, desire it.

ALITHEA (*Aside*)

So 'twill be in other things, I warrant.   100

MRS PINCHWIFE

Pray, let me go to a play, dear.

PINCHWIFE

Hold your peace, I won't.

MRS PINCHWIFE

Why, love?

PINCHWIFE

Why, I'll tell you.

ALITHEA (*Aside*)

Nay, if he tell her, she'll give him more cause forbid her   105
that place.

MRS PINCHWIFE

Pray, why, dear?

PINCHWIFE

First, you like the actors, and the gallants may like you.

MRS PINCHWIFE

What, a homely country girl? No, bud, nobody will like
me.   110

---

93   sp MRS PINCHWIFE Q1–5, O. Gamini Salgado assigns this speech to Alithea (*Three Restoration Comedies*, 1968). But if Mrs Pinchwife has it Pinchwife's question (l. 94) makes better
sense.

PINCHWIFE

I tell you, yes, they may.

MRS PINCHWIFE

No, no, you jest – I won't believe you, I will go.

PINCHWIFE

I tell you then, that one of the lewdest fellows in town, who saw you there, told me he was in love with you.

MRS PINCHWIFE

Indeed! Who, who, pray who was't?   115

PINCHWIFE (*Aside*)

I've gone too far, and slipped before I was aware. How overjoyed she is!

MRS PINCHWIFE

Was it any Hampshire gallant, any of our neighbours? I promise you, I am beholding to him.

PINCHWIFE

I promise you, you lie; for he would but ruin you, as he   120
has done hundreds. He has no other love for women, but that; such as he look upon women like basilisks, but to destroy 'em.

MRS PINCHWIFE

Ay, but if he loves me, why should he ruin me? Answer me to that. Methinks he should not; I would do him no   125
harm.

ALITHEA

Ha, ha, ha!

PINCHWIFE

'Tis very well; but I'll keep him from doing you any harm, or me either.

Enter SPARKISH *and* HARCOURT

But here comes company; get you in, get you in.   130

MRS PINCHWIFE

But pray, husband, is he a pretty gentleman that loves me?

---

119 *beholding* beholden
122 *like basilisks* as basilisks do, a basilisk being a fabulous reptile whose glance was fatal

PINCHWIFE

> In, baggage, in! (*Thrusts her in; shuts the door*) [*Aside*] What, all
> the lewd libertines of the town brought to my lodging by this
> easy coxcomb! 'Sdeath, I'll not suffer it.   135

SPARKISH

> Here Harcourt, do you approve my choice? [*To* ALITHEA] Dear
> little rogue, I told you I'd bring you acquainted with all my friends,
> the wits, and –
>
>   HARCOURT *salutes her*

PINCHWIFE [*Aside*]

> Ay, they shall know her, as well as you yourself will, I warrant
> you.   140

SPARKISH

> This is one of those, my pretty rogue, that are to dance at
> your wedding tomorrow; and him you must bid welcome ever
> to what you and I have.

PINCHWIFE (*Aside*)

> Monstrous!

SPARKISH

> Harcourt, how dost thou like her, faith? – Nay, dear, do not   145
> look down; I should hate to have a wife of mine out of
> countenance at anything.

PINCHWIFE [*Aside*]

> Wonderful!

SPARKISH

> Tell me, I say, Harcourt, how dost thou like her? Thou hast
> stared upon her enough to resolve me.   150

HARCOURT

> So infinitely well that I could wish I had a mistress too, that
> might differ from her in nothing but her love and engagement
> to you.

ALITHEA

> Sir, Master Sparkish has often told me that his
> acquaintance were all wits and railleurs, and now I find   155
> it.

---

135 *easy coxcomb* easy-going fop
150 *resolve me* give me your opinion
155 *railleurs* railers, mockers; fashionable French word likely to have been used by Sparkish.
        See I.i. 287.

SPARKISH

No, by the universe madam, he does not rally now;
you may believe him, I do assure you, he is the honestest,
worthiest, true-hearted gentleman – a man of such,
perfect honour, he would say nothing to a lady he does not   160
mean.

PINCHWIFE [*Aside*]

Praising another man to his mistress!

HARCOURT

Sir, you are so beyond expectation obliging, that –

SPARKISH

Nay, i'gad, I am sure you do admire her extremely; I see't in
your eyes. – He does admire you, madam. – By the world,   165
don't you?

HARCOURT

Yes, above the world, or the most glorious part of it, her
whole sex; and till now I never thought I should have envied
you or any man about to marry, but you have the best excuse for
marriage I ever knew.   170

ALITHEA

Nay, now, sir, I'm satisfied you are of the society of the wits
and railleurs since you cannot spare your friend even when he
is but too civil to you. But the surest sign is, since you are an
enemy to marriage; for that, I hear, you hate as much as business
or bad wine.   175

HARCOURT

Truly, madam, I never was an enemy to marriage till
now, because marriage was never an enemy to me
before.

ALITHEA

But why, sir, is marriage an enemy to you now? Because it
robs you of your friend here? For you look upon a friend   180
married as one gone into a monastery, that is dead to the
world.

173–5 Raillery against marriage was so common among the wits as to have become unfashionable; Friedman quotes Thomas Shadwell, *The Miser* (1672), where Bellmour complains
of Hazard that he has 'the common place wit of all the young fops in this town, in railing
against marriage'.

HARCOURT

'Tis indeed, because you marry him; I see, madam, you can guess my meaning. I do confess heartily and openly, I wish it were in my power to break the match. By heavens I would!   185

SPARKISH

Poor Frank!

ALITHEA

Would you be so unkind to me?

HARCOURT

No, no, 'tis not because I would be unkind to you.

SPARKISH

Poor Frank! No, gad, 'tis only his kindness to me.   190

PINCHWIFE (*Aside*)

Great kindness to you indeed! Insensible fop, let a man make love to his wife to his face!

SPARKISH

Come, dear Frank, for all my wife there that shall be, thou shalt enjoy me sometimes, dear rogue. By my honour, we men of wit condole for our deceased brother in marriage as much as for one dead in earnest. – I think that was prettily said of me, ha, Harcourt? – But come, Frank, be not melancholy for me.   195

HARCOURT

No, I assure you I am not melancholy for you.

SPARKISH

Prithee, Frank, dost think my wife that shall be, there, a fine person?   200

HARCOURT

I could gaze upon her till I became as blind as you are.

SPARKISH

How, as I am? How?

HARCOURT

Because you are a lover, and true lovers are blind, stock blind.   205

194   *enjoy me* have the pleasure of my company
198   *not* Q2–5, O (not not Q1)
204–5   *stock blind* as blind as a lifeless thing or stupid person (*OED* stock sb¹. VIII. 60)

SPARKISH

True, true; but by the world, she has wit too, as well as beauty.
Go, go with her into a corner, and try if she has wit; talk to her
anything; she's bashful before me.

HARCOURT

Indeed, if a woman wants wit in a corner, she has it
nowhere.   210

ALITHEA (*Aside to* SPARKISH)

Sir, you dispose of me a little before your time –

SPARKISH

Nay, nay, madam, let me have an earnest of your obedience
or – Go, go, madam –

                                    HARCOURT *courts* ALITHEA *aside*

PINCHWIFE

How, sir! If you are not concerned for the honour of
a wife, I am for that of a sister; he shall not debauch her.   215
Be a pander to your own wife, bring men to her, let 'em
make love before your face, thrust 'em into a corner together,
then leave 'em in private! Is this your town wit and
conduct?

SPARKISH

Ha, ha, ha! A silly wise rogue would make one laugh more than a   220
stark fool, ha, ha! I shall burst. Nay, you shall not disturb 'em; I'll
vex thee, by the world.

                                    Struggles with PINCHWIFE *to keep him*
                                    from HARCOURT *and* ALITHEA

ALITHEA

The writings are drawn, sir, settlements made; 'tis too late, sir,
and past all revocation.

HARCOURT

Then so is my death.   225

---

209   *wit in a corner* i.e., perhaps, impudence in an assignation. In *Love in a Wood* Lady Flip-
        pant complains 'I do not know a man of you all, that will not thrust a woman up into a
        corner, and then talk an hour to her impertinently of marriage', and Ranger assures her
        'You would find me another man in a corner' (I.ii.261–4). A distant echo of Horace, *Odes*,
        'gratus puellae risus ab angulo' (1.9.22), the agreeable laughter of a girl from a
        corner.
212   *earnest* foretaste
220   *would* who would
222   *vex* thwart

ALITHEA

I would not be unjust to him.

HARCOURT

Then why to me so?

ALITHEA

I have no obligation to you.

HARCOURT

My love.

ALITHEA

I had his before.   230

HARCOURT

You never had it; he wants, you see, jealousy, the only
infallible sign of it.

ALITHEA

Love proceeds from esteem; he cannot distrust my virtue. Besides
he loves me, or he would not marry me.

HARCOURT

Marrying you is no more sign of his love, than bribing   235
your woman, that he may marry you, is a sign of his
generosity. Marriage is rather a sign of interest than love; and
he that marries a fortune, covets a mistress, not loves her. But if
you take marriage for a sign of love, take it from me
immediately.   240

ALITHEA

No, now you have put a scruple in my head. But in short, sir,
to end our dispute, I must marry him; my reputation would
suffer in the world else.

HARCOURT

No, if you do marry him, with your pardon, madam, your
reputation suffers in the world, and you would be thought in   245
necessity for a cloak.

ALITHEA

Nay, now you are rude, sir. – Master Sparkish, pray come
hither, your friend here is very troublesome, and very
loving.

231–2 proverbial, and a recurrent idea in Wycherley. See *Love in a Wood* IV.iii. 28–9.
  237 *interest* self-interest
        than Q4–5, O (then Q1–3)
  246 *cloak* cover for immorality. Cook and Swannell quote Aphra Behn, *The City Heiress* (1682):
        'Would you have the impudence to marry an old coxcomb, a fellow that will not so much
        as serve you for a cloak, he is so visibly and undeniably impotent?' (II.iii). See also III.ii.190.

[71]

HARCOURT (*Aside to* ALITHEA)

Hold, hold!   250

PINCHWIFE

D'ye hear that?

SPARKISH

Why, d'ye think I'll seem to be jealous, like a country bumpkin?

PINCHWIFE

No, rather be a cuckold, like a credulous cit.

HARCOURT

Madam, you would not have been so little generous as to   255
have told him?

ALITHEA

Yes, since you could be so little generous as to wrong him.

HARCOURT

Wrong him! No man can do't, he's beneath an injury; a bubble, a coward, a senseless idiot, a wretch so contemptible   260
to all the world but you that –

ALITHEA

Hold, do not rail at him, for since he is like to be my husband I am resolved to like him. Nay, I think I am obliged to tell him you are not his friend. – Master Sparkish, Master Sparkish!   265

SPARKISH

What, what? Now, dear rogue, has not she wit?

HARCOURT (*Speaks surlily*)

Not so much as I thought, and hoped she had.

ALITHEA

Master Sparkish, do you bring people to rail at you?

HARCOURT

Madam –

SPARKISH

How! No, but if he does rail at me, 'tis but in jest, I warrant;   270
what we wits do for one another and never take any notice of it.

---

254   *cit* citizen; disparaging
260   *bubble* dupe. See also III.ii. 64–72.

ALITHEA

He spoke so scurrilously of you, I had no patience to hear
him; besides, he has been making love to me.

HARCOURT (*Aside*)

True, damned, tell-tale woman.   275

SPARKISH

Pshaw! to show his parts. We wits rail and make love often
but to show our parts; as we have no affections, so we have no
malice; we –

ALITHEA

He said you were a wretch, below an injury.

SPARKISH

Pshaw!   280

HARCOURT [*Aside*]

Damned, senseless, impudent, virtuous jade! Well, since
she won't let me have her, she'll do as good, she'll make me
hate her.

ALITHEA

A common bubble.

SPARKISH

Pshaw!   285

ALITHEA

A coward.

SPARKISH

Pshaw, pshaw!

ALITHEA

A senseless, drivelling idiot.

SPARKISH

How! Did he disparage my parts? Nay, then my honour's
concerned. I can't put up that, sir, by the world. Brother,   290
help me to kill him. (*Aside*) I may draw now, since we have
the odds of him. 'Tis a good occasion, too, before my
mistress –   *Offers to draw*

---

276 *parts* (generally) talents, intellectual abilities; (to fops like Sparkish) superficial accom-
plishments; (sometimes) private parts. The bawdy *double entendre* follows at ll. 277 and
289–90, but maybe Sparkish does not know what he is saying, like Sir Jaspar Fidget at
II.i.602 and IV.iii.105, 148–9.

289 *disparage my parts* criticise my intellectual power, 'say . . . I am a fool, that is no wit'
(l. 304)

290 *put up* put up with

ALITHEA

Hold, hold!

SPARKISH

What, what?   295

ALITHEA (*Aside*)

I must not let 'em kill the gentleman neither, for his
kindness to me; I am so far from hating him that I wish my
gallant had his person and understanding. – Nay, if my
honour –

SPARKISH

I'll be thy death.   300

ALITHEA

Hold, hold! Indeed, to tell the truth, the gentleman said
after all that what he spoke was but out of friendship to
you.

SPARKISH

How! say, I am – I am a fool, that is no wit, out of friendship
to me?   305

ALITHEA

Yes, to try whether I was concerned enough for you, and
made love to me only to be satisfied of my virtue, for your
sake.

HARCOURT (*Aside*)

Kind, however –

SPARKISH

Nay, if it were so, my dear rogue, I ask thee pardon. But why   310
would not you tell me so, faith?

HARCOURT

Because I did not think on't, faith.

SPARKISH

Come, Horner does not come. Harcourt, let's be gone to the
new play. – Come, madam.

ALITHEA

I will not go, if you intend to leave me alone in the box and   315
run into the pit, as you use to do.

302 *after all* in conclusion
304 *I am* the repetition may be a printer's error, but seems to be a dramatic device, as in
      similar cases at ll. 557–8 and 562–3 below and at V.iii. 77.
315 *box* one of a number of private boxes in the theatre gallery
316 *pit* where 'the wits' row' (I.i. 310) was

SPARKISH

Pshaw! I'll leave Harcourt with you in the box to entertain
you and that's as good. If I sat in the box I should be
thought no judge but of trimmings. – Come away, Harcourt, lead
her down.   320

Exeunt SPARKISH, HARCOURT *and* ALITHEA

PINCHWIFE

Well, go thy ways, for the flower of the true town fops,
such as spend their estates before they come to 'em, and are
cuckolds before they're married. But let me go look to my
own freehold – How!

Enter my LADY FIDGET, *Mrs* DAINTY FIDGET
and Mrs SQUEAMISH

LADY FIDGET

Your servant, sir. Where is your lady? We are come to wait   325
upon her to the new play.

PINCHWIFE

New play!

LADY FIDGET

And my husband will wait upon you presently.

PINCHWIFE (*Aside*)

Damn your civility. – Madam, by no means; I will not see
Sir Jaspar here till I have waited upon him at home; nor   330
shall my wife see you till she has waited upon your ladyship at
your lodgings.

LADY FIDGET

Now we are here, sir –

PINCHWIFE

No, madam.

DAINTY

Pray let us see her.   335

SQUEAMISH

We will not stir till we see her.

---

319 *trimmings* probably, fashionable adornments. See I.i.283
319–20 *lead her down* give her your arm
324 *freehold* i.e. his wife

PINCHWIFE (*Aside*)

A pox on you all! (*Goes to the door and returns*) She has
locked the door, and is gone abroad.

LADY FIDGET

No, you have locked the door, and she's within.

DAINTY

They told us below, she was here.   340

PINCHWIFE [*Aside*]

Will nothing do? – Well, it must out then. To tell you the
truth, ladies, which I was afraid to let you know before, lest it
might endanger your lives, my wife has just now the
small-pox come out upon her. Do not be frightened; but pray,
be gone, ladies; you shall not stay here in danger of your lives;   345
pray get you gone, ladies.

LADY FIDGET

No, no, we have all had 'em.

SQUEAMISH

Alack, alack!

DAINTY

Come, come, we must see how it goes with her; I understand
the disease.   350

LADY FIDGET

Come.

PINCHWIFE (*Aside*)

Well, there is no being too hard for women at their own weapon,
lying; therefore I'll quit the field.   *Exit* PINCHWIFE

SQUEAMISH

Here's an example of jealousy!

LADY FIDGET

Indeed, as the world goes, I wonder there are no more jealous,   355
since wives are so neglected.

DAINTY

Pshaw! as the world goes, to what end should they be
jealous?

LADY FIDGET

Foh! 'tis a nasty world.

357–8   i.e. they need not be jealous, since wives are neglected by lovers as well as by
husbands

SQUEAMISH

That men of parts, great acquaintance, and quality should   360
take up with and spend themselves and fortunes in keeping
little playhouse creatures, foh!

LADY FIDGET

Nay, that women of understanding, great acquaintance
and good quality should fall a-keeping, too, of little creatures,
foh!   365

SQUEAMISH

Why, 'tis the men of quality's fault. They never visit women of
honour and reputation as they used to do; and have not so
much as common civility for ladies of our rank, but use us
with the same indifferency and ill-breeding as if we were all
married to 'em.   370

LADY FIDGET

She says true! 'Tis an arrant shame women of quality should
be so slighted. Methinks, birth – birth should go for something.
I have known men admired, courted, and followed for their
titles only.

SQUEAMISH

Ay, one would think men of honour should not love, no more   375
than marry, out of their own rank.

DAINTY

Fie, fie upon 'em! They are come to think cross-breeding
for themselves best, as well as for their dogs and
horses.

LADY FIDGET

They are dogs, and horses for't.   380

SQUEAMISH

One would think, if not for love, for vanity a little.

DAINTY

Nay, they do satisfy their vanity upon us sometimes,
and are kind to us in their report; tell all the world they
lie with us.

360–2 Nell Gwyn was only the most famous actress who took up such an offer. See also
      Prologue, ll. 27–8.
363–5 For instance, Lady Castlemaine had liaisons with both Charles Hart and Wycherley him-
      self.
  369 *indifferency* indifference
375–6 *love, no more than marry,* ed. (love no more, than marry Q1–5, O)
  380 *for't* for thinking it.

LADY FIDGET

Damned rascals! That we should be only wronged by 'em.   385
To report a man has had a person, when he has not had a
person, is the greatest wrong in the whole world that can be
done to a person.

SQUEAMISH

Well, 'tis an arrant shame noble persons should be so
wronged and neglected.   390

LADY FIDGET

But still 'tis an arranter shame for a noble person to neglect her
own honour, and defame her own noble person with little
inconsiderable fellows, foh!

DAINTY

I suppose the crime against our honour is the same with a
man of quality as with another.   395

LADY FIDGET

How! No, sure, the man of quality is likest one's husband and
therefore the fault should be the less.

DAINTY

But then the pleasure should be the less.

LADY FIDGET

Fie, fie, fie, for shame, sister! Whither shall we ramble? Be
continent in your discourse, or I shall hate you.   400

DAINTY

Besides, an intrigue is so much the more notorious for the
man's quality.

SQUEAMISH

'Tis true, nobody takes notice of a private man, and therefore
with him 'tis more secret, and the crime's the less when 'tis
not known.   405

---

399   *ramble* allow our lascivious thoughts to wander. John D. Patterson, 'The Restoration
       Ramble', *Notes and Queries* vol. 226 (1981), 209–10, notes that at this time the verb often
       meant 'go out in search of sex', quoting Wycherley's *Love in a Wood* among other sources.
400   *in your discourse,* i.e., in your discourse at least
403   *private* without rank in society
404–5 *the crime's the less when 'tis not known* a libertine commonplace; 'To be taken, to be seen, /
       These have crimes accounted been' Jonson, *Volpone* III.vii. 181–2)

LADY FIDGET

You say true. I'faith, I think you are in the right on't. 'Tis not
an injury to a husband till it be an injury to our honours; so that
a woman of honour loses no honour with a private person;
and to say truth –

DAINTY (*Apart to* SQUEAMISH)

So, the little fellow is grown a private person – with her.   410

LADY FIDGET

But still my dear, dear honour.

Enter SIR JASPAR, HORNER, DORILANT

SIR JASPAR

Ay, my dear, dear of honour, thou hast still so much honour
in thy mouth –

HORNER (*Aside*)

That she has none elsewhere.

LADY FIDGET

Oh, what d'ye mean to bring in these upon us?   415

DAINTY

Foh! these are as bad as wits.

SQUEAMISH

Foh!

LADY FIDGET

Let us leave the room.

SIR JASPAR

Stay, stay; faith, to tell you the naked truth

LADY FIDGET

Fie, Sir Jaspar, do not use that word 'naked'.   420

SIR JASPAR

Well, well, in short, I have business at Whitehall, and
cannot go to the play with you, therefore would have you
go –

LADY FIDGET

With those two to a play?

---

412 *dear of honour* dear to me because of your virtue
416 *as bad as wits* who were notorious for ribaldry and debauchery
421 *Whitehall* i.e., at court. See I.i. 98 and introduction, p. 6.

SIR JASPAR

No, not with t'other but with Master Horner. There can be no   425
more scandal to go with him than with Master Tattle, or Master
Limberham.

LADY FIDGET

With that nasty fellow! No – no!

SIR JASPAR

Nay, prithee dear, hear me.   *Whispers to* LADY FIDGET

HORNER

Ladies –   430

      HORNER, DORILANT *drawing near* SQUEAMISH *and* DAINTY

DAINTY

Stand off!

SQUEAMISH

Do not approach us!

DAINTY

You herd with the wits, you are obscenity all over.

SQUEAMISH

And I would as soon look upon a picture of Adam and
Eve, without fig leaves, as any of you, if I could help it, therefore   435
keep off, and do not make us sick.

DORILANT

What a devil are these?

HORNER

Why, these are pretenders to honour, as critics to wit,
only by censuring others; and as every raw, peevish, out-
of-humoured, affected, dull, tea-drinking, arithmetical fop   440
sets up for a wit, by railing at men of sense, so these for
honour by railing at the court and ladies of as great honour as
quality.

426–7 *Master Tattle, or Master Limberham* names probably of the 'two old civil gentlemen' men-
      tioned at II.i.496, *Tattle* suggesting idle talk, *Limberham* obsequiousness. Wycherley
      apparently invented the name Limberham, borrowed by Dryden for a 'tame, foolish
      keeper' in *The Kind Keeper; or, Mr Limberham* (1678). Tattle was used by Congreve for a
      fop in *Love for Love* (1695).

429   sd Sir Jaspar has already told his wife Horner is a eunuch (I.i. 92), but the context
      suggests that is what he whispers about here. The effect is to leave centre stage for the
      comic exchange between the wits and the other ladies.

437   *What a devil* what the devil

440   *arithmetical* excessively precise; not recorded in this sense in *OED*

SIR JASPAR
Come, Master Horner, I must desire you to go with these
ladies to the play, sir.   445

HORNER
I, sir?

SIR JASPAR
Ay, ay, come, sir.

HORNER
I must beg your pardon, sir, and theirs. I will not be seen
in women's company in public again for the world.

SIR JASPAR
Ha, ha! strange aversion!   450

SQUEAMISH
No, he's for women's company in private.

SIR JASPAR
He – poor man – he! ha, ha, ha!

DAINTY
'Tis a greater shame amongst lewd fellows to be seen in
virtuous women's company than for the women to be seen
with them.   455

HORNER
Indeed, madam, the time was I only hated virtuous
women, but now I hate the other too; I beg your pardon,
ladies.

LADY FIDGET
You are very obliging, sir, because we would not be troubled
with you.   460

SIR JASPAR
In sober sadness, he shall go.

DORILANT
Nay, if he won't, I am ready to wait upon the ladies; and I think
I am the fitter man.

SIR JASPAR
You, sir? No, I thank you for that. Master Horner is a privileged
man amongst the virtuous ladies; 'twill be a great while before   465
you are so, he, he, he! He's my wife's gallant, he, he, he! No,
pray withdraw, sir, for as I take it, the virtuous ladies have no
business with you.

---

461   *in sober sadness* in all seriousness; perhaps an old-fashioned asseveration

DORILANT

    And I am sure he can have none with them. 'Tis strange a
    man can't come amongst virtuous women now, but upon the   470
    same terms as men are admitted into the great Turk's seraglio;
    but heavens keep me from being an ombre player with 'em! But
    where is Pinchwife?   *Exit* DORILANT

SIR JASPAR

    Come, come, man; what, avoid the sweet society of woman-kind? –
    that sweet, soft, gentle, tame, noble creature, woman, made   475
    for man's companion –

HORNER

    So is that soft, gentle, tame, and more noble creature a
    spaniel, and has all their tricks; can fawn, lie down, suffer
    beating, and fawn the more; barks at your friends when they
    come to see you; makes your bed hard; gives you fleas,   480
    and the mange sometimes. And all the difference is, the
    spaniel's the more faithful animal and fawns but upon one
    master.

SIR JASPAR

    He, he, he!

SQUEAMISH

    Oh, the rude beast!   485

DAINTY

    Insolent brute!

LADY FIDGET

    Brute! Stinking, mortified, rotten French wether, to
    dare –

SIR JASPAR

    Hold, an't please your ladyship. – For shame, Master
    Horner, your mother was a woman. – (*Aside*) Now shall   490
    I never reconcile 'em. – Hark you, madam, take my
    advice in your anger. You know you often want one to

471 *great Turk* Sultan of Turkey; mentioned again at IV.iii. 358
472 *ombre* card game said to have made fashionable by Charles II's wife Catherine of
    Braganza. From the Spanish *juego del hombre*, the man's game. So Dorilant is saying both
    that he does not want to play cards with the ladies and that he does not want to play at
    being a man with them. See similar pun at IV.iii. 215–17.
487 *mortified, rotten French wether* literally, tenderised but rotten meat of a castrated ram;
    OED 5 quoting Fynes Moryson, *An Itinerary* (1617), 'The French alone delight in morti-
    fied meats' (III. 134); metaphorically, man made impotent by the pox

make up your drolling pack of ombre players; and you may
cheat him easily, for he's an ill gamester, and consequently
loves play. Besides, you know, you have but two   495
old civil gentlemen (with stinking breaths too) to wait
upon you abroad; take in the third into your service.
The other are but crazy; and a lady should have a
supernumerary gentleman-usher, as a supernumerary
coachhorse, lest sometimes you should be forced to stay   500
at home.

LADY FIDGET

But are you sure he loves play, and has money?

SIR JASPAR

He loves play as much as you, and has money as much as I.

LADY FIDGET

Then I am contented to make him pay for his scurrility;
money makes up in a measure all other wants in men. – (*Aside*)   505
Those whom we cannot make hold for gallants, we
make fine.

SIR JASPAR (*Aside*)

So, so; now to mollify, to wheedle him. – Master
Horner, will you never keep civil company? Methinks
'tis time now, since you are only fit for them. Come, come,   510
man, you must e'en fall to visiting our wives, eating at
our tables, drinking tea with our virtuous relations
after dinner, dealing cards to 'em, reading plays and
gazettes to 'em, picking fleas out of their shocks for 'em,

---

493 *drolling* ridiculous
494 *gamester* gambler
495 *play* gambling
498 *other* others; *but crazy* almost ga-ga
499 *gentleman usher* attendant on a person of rank. They were going out of fashion, as Etherege
     suggests: *The Man of Mode* (1676) I.i. 67–9.
     as as she would have
506 *make hold for* occupy the position of
507 *make fine* require to pay. But as a *fine* was often a payment to avoid the duties of office,
     there is probably a satirical reference to Horner's presumed impotence.
508 *wheedle* win over. See also l. 540.
512 *drinking tea* harmless custom especially hateful to Horner. See l.440
514 *gazettes* newspapers
     shocks poodles

collecting receipts, new songs, women, pages, and footmen   515
for 'em.

SIR JASPAR

He, he, he! 'Tis fit you know your work before you come
into your place; and since you are unprovided of a lady
to flatter, and a good house to eat at, pray frequent mine, and   520
call my wife mistress, and she shall call you gallant, according to
the custom.

HORNER

Who, I?

SIR JASPAR

Faith, thou shalt for my sake; come, for my sake only.

HORNER

For your sake –   525

SIR JASPAR

Come, come, here's a gamester for you; let him be a little
familiar sometimes; nay, what if a little rude? Gamesters may
be rude with ladies, you know.

LADY FIDGET

Yes, losing gamesters have a privilege with women.

HORNER

I always thought the contrary, that the winning gamester had most   530
privilege with women; for when you have lost your money to a
man, you'll lose anything you have, all you have, they say, and he
may use you as he pleases.

SIR JASPAR

He, he, he! Well, win or lose, you shall have your liberty
with her.   535

LADY FIDGET

As he behaves himself; and for your sake I'll give him
admittance and freedom.

---

515 *receipts* recipes
      women waiting women
521–2 The custom is observed by Lady Fidget and Horner, ll. 604–5 (and by the somewhat
      similarly related Lucy and Gripe, *Love in a Wood* V.i. 151–2). The words *mistress* and *gal-*
      lant could be more or less innocent; Friedman quotes Thomas Blount, *Glossographia*
      (1670): 'Gallant . . . Servant or Platonick to a Lady' (p. 287).
526 *gamester* gambler, as at l. 494. But the slang sense, 'wencher', could also be intended.

HORNER

All sorts of freedom, madam?

SIR JASPAR

Ay, ay, ay, all sorts of freedom thou canst take, and so go to
her, begin thy new employment; wheedle her, jest with her, and be   540
better acquainted one with another.

HORNER (*Aside*)

I think I know her already, therefore may venture with her,
my secret for hers.

> HORNER *and* LADY FIDGET *whisper*

SIR JASPAR

Sister, cuz, I have provided an innocent playfellow for
you there.   545

DAINTY

Who, he?

SQUEAMISH

There's a playfellow indeed!

SIR JASPAR

Yes, sure, what, he is good enough to play at cards, blind
man's buff, or the fool with sometimes.

SQUEAMISH

Foh! we'll have no such playfellows.   550

DAINTY

No, sir, you shan't choose playfellows for us, we thank
you.

SIR JASPAR

Nay, pray hear me.   *Whispering to them*

LADY FIDGET

But, poor gentleman, could you be so generous, so truly a
man of honour, as for the sakes of us women of honour,   555
to cause yourself to be reported no man? No man! And
to suffer yourself the greatest shame that could fall upon
a man, that none might fall upon us women by your
conversation? But indeed, sir, as perfectly, perfectly, the

---

542 *venture* Q2–5, O (venter Q1, probably just alternative spelling), bargain
544 *cuz* abbreviation of cousin, used in familiar address, especially to relatives
547 *playfellow* sexual partner; *double entendre*. See Farmer and Henley under 'play' and Partridge, *Shakespeare's Bawdy* (1968), p.162.
553 sd Presumably he tells them Horner is a eunuch, while Horner assures Lady Fidget he is not.
559 *conversation* intercourse; *double entendre*

[85]

same man as before your going into France, sir? As perfectly,   560
perfectly, sir?

HORNER

As perfectly, perfectly, madam. Nay, I scorn you should take my
word; I desire to be tried only, madam.

LADY FIDGET

Well, that's spoken again like a man of honour; all
men of honour desire to come to the test. But, indeed,   565
generally, you men report such things of yourselves, one does
not know how or whom to believe; and it is come to that
pass, we dare not take your words no more than your
tailors, without some staid servant of yours be bound with
you. But I have so strong a faith in your honour, dear,   570
dear, noble sir, that I'd forfeit mine for yours at any time,
dear sir.

HORNER

No, madam, you should not need to forfeit it for me.
I have given you security already to save you harmless,
my late reputation being so well known in the world,   575
madam.

LADY FIDGET

But if upon any future falling out, or upon a suspicion
of my taking the trust out of your hands, to employ some
other, you yourself should betray your trust, dear sir? I
mean, if you'll give me leave to speak obscenely, you might tell,   580
dear sir.

HORNER

If I did, nobody would believe me; the reputation of impotency is
as hardly recovered again in the world as that of cowardice,
dear madam.

LADY FIDGET

Nay, then, as one may say, you may do your worst, dear,   585
dear, sir.

568–9 *no more than your tailors* any more than your tailors would
  569 *staid* settled in character
    be bound literally, stand surety for payment (to the tailor); metaphorically perhaps, give
    sexual satisfaction (if the gallant does not)
  574 *save you harmless* save you from harm (by scandal); legal terminology (Dixon)
  580 *obscenely* Characteristically, she associates plain dealing with indecency – though she
    may be joking.
  583 *recovered again* recovered from

SIR JASPAR

Come, is your ladyship reconciled to him yet? Have you agreed
on matters? For I must be gone to Whitehall.

LADY FIDGET

Why, indeed, Sir Jaspar, Master Horner is a thousand,
thousand times a better man than I thought him.   590
Cousin Squeamish, Sister Dainty, I can name him now,
truly; not long ago, you know, I thought his very name
obscenity, and I would as soon have lain with him as have
named him.

SIR JASPAR

Very likely, poor madam.   595

DAINTY

I believe it.

SQUEAMISH

No doubt on't.

SIR JASPAR

Well, well, that your ladyship is as virtuous as any she, I
know, and him all the town knows, he, he, he! Therefore,
now you like him, get you gone to your business together;   600
go, go, to your business, I say, pleasure, whilst I go to my pleasure,
business.

LADY FIDGET

Come then, dear gallant.

HORNER

Come away, my dearest mistress.

SIR JASPAR

So, so; why 'tis as I'd have it.   *Exit* SIR JASPAR   605

HORNER

And as I'd have it.

LADY FIDGET

Who for his business, from his wife will run,
Takes the best care, to have her business done.

Exeunt omnes

---

601   *business* both frivolous activity and sexual intercourse. Sir Jaspar intends the first irony,
but not the second. Lady Fidget makes the bawdy meaning quite clear in l. 608 below.

605   It is as Sir Jaspar would have it partly because Lady Fidget and Horner are using the terms
he suggested (ll. 521) – but not in the senses he intended.

Act III, Scene i

ALITHEA *and* MRS PINCHWIFE

ALITHEA
Sister, what ails you? You are grown melancholy.

MRS PINCHWIFE
Would it not make anyone melancholy, to see you go every day
fluttering about abroad, whilst I must stay at home like a poor
lonely sullen bird in a cage?

ALITHEA
Ay, sister, but you came young and just from the nest to your   5
cage, so that I thought you liked it; and could be as cheerful
in't as others that took their flight themselves early, and are
hopping abroad in the open air.

MRS PINCHWIFE
Nay, I confess I was quiet enough till my husband told me
what pure lives the London ladies live abroad, with their dancing,   10
meetings, and junketings, and dressed every day in their best
gowns; and I warrant you, play at ninepins every day of the
week, so they do.

Enter PINCHWIFE

PINCHWIFE
Come, what's here to do? You are putting the town pleasures
in her head, and setting her a-longing.   15

ALITHEA
Yes, after ninepins! You suffer none to give her those longings
you mean, but yourself.

PINCHWIFE
I tell her of the vanities of the town like a confessor.

ALITHEA
A confessor! Just such a confessor as he that, by forbidding
a silly ostler to grease the horse's teeth, taught him   20
to do't.

---

10 *pure* wonderful; childish or vulgar term
12 *ninepins* a game 'still kept in action by the bumpkins', according to Francis Kirkman, *The
    Unlucky Citizen* (1673), p. 10; unlikely to have been played by the London ladies
20–1 Sophisticated ostlers used grease to inhibit feeding, and so make a better profit on the
    provender.

PINCHWIFE

Come, Mistress Flippant, good precepts are lost when bad
examples are still before us. The liberty you take abroad
makes her hanker after it, and out of humour at home.
Poor wretch! she desired not to come to London; I would   25
bring her.

ALITHEA

Very well.

PINCHWIFE

She has been this week in town, and never desired, till this
afternoon, to go abroad.

ALITHEA

Was she not at a play yesterday?   30

PINCHWIFE

Yes, but she ne'er asked me. I was myself the cause of
her going.

ALITHEA

Then, if she ask you again, you are the cause of her asking,
and not my example.

PINCHWIFE

Well, tomorrow night I shall be rid of you; and the next   35
day, before 'tis light, she and I'll be rid of the town, and
my dreadful apprehensions. Come, be not melancholy,
for thou shalt go into the country after tomorrow,
dearest.

ALITHEA

Great comfort!   40

MRS PINCHWIFE

Pish! what d'ye tell me of the country for?

PINCHWIFE

How's this? What, pish at the country?

MRS PINCHWIFE

Let me alone, I am not well.

PINCHWIFE

O, if that be all – what ails my dearest?

MRS PINCHWIFE

Truly I don't know; but I have not been well since you told   45
me there was a gallant at the play in love with me.

---

22 *Mistress Flippant* Lady Flippant was a hypocritical character in *Love in a Wood*; the word
    means 'impertinently voluble' (*OED* 2.b).

PINCHWIFE

Ha!

ALITHEA

That's by my example, too!

PINCHWIFE

Nay, if you are not well, but are so concerned because a
lewd fellow chanced to lie and say he liked you, you'll make   50
me sick too.

MRS PINCHWIFE

Of what sickness?

PINCHWIFE

O, of that which is worse than the plague – jealousy.

MRS PINCHWIFE

Pish, you jeer! I'm sure there's no such disease in our receipt-
book at home.   55

PINCHWIFE

No thou never met'st with it, poor innocent. (*Aside*)
Well, if thou cuckold me, 'twill be my own fault, for
cuckolds and bastards are generally makers of their own
fortune.

MRS PINCHWIFE

Well , but pray, bud, let's go to a play tonight   60

PINCHWIFE

'Tis just done, she comes from it; but why are you so eager
to see a play?

MRS PINCHWIFE

Faith dear, not that I care one pin for their talk there,
but I like to look upon the player-men, and would
see, if I could, the gallant you say loves me; that's all, dear   65
bud.

PINCHWIFE

Is that all, dear bud?

ALITHEA

This proceeds from my example.

54 *you jeer* you are joking; expression frequently used by Mrs Pinchwife
57–9 'The wary fool is by his care betrayed, / As cuckolds by their jealousy are made' (*The
Gentleman Dancing-Master* III.i. 595–6)
61 *'Tis just done* i.e., it is early evening, as plays were performed in the late afternoon

MRS PINCHWIFE

But if the play be done, let's go abroad, however, dear
bud.   70

PINCHWIFE

Come, have a little patience, and thou shalt go into the
country on Friday.

MRS PINCHWIFE

Therefore I would see first some sights, to tell my neighbours
of. Nay, I will go abroad, that's once.

ALITHEA

I'm the cause of this desire too.   75

PINCHWIFE

But now I think on't, who was the cause of Horner's coming
to my lodging today? That was you.

ALITHEA

No, you, because you would not let him see your handsome
wife out of your lodging.

MRS PINCHWIFE

Why, O Lord! Did the gentleman come hither to see me   80
indeed?

PINCHWIFE

No, no. – You are not cause of that damned question
too, Mistress Alithea? (*Aside*) Well, she's in the right of it.
He is in love with my wife – and comes after her – 'tis so –
but I'll nip his love in the bud; lest he should follow us into   85
the country and break his chariot-wheel near our house on
purpose for an excuse to come to't. But I think I know
the town.

MRS PINCHWIFE

Come, pray bud, let's go abroad before 'tis late. For I will go,
that's flat and plain.   90

PINCHWIFE (*Aside*)

So! the obstinacy already of a town-wife, and I must, whilst
she's here, humour her like one. – Sister, how shall we do, that she
may not be seen or known?

ALITHEA

Let her put on her mask.

---

74   *that's once* that's flat; vulgarism
86   *chariot* carriage

PINCHWIFE

Pshaw! A mask makes people but the more inquisitive, and   95
is as ridiculous a disguise as a stage beard; her shape, stature,
habit will be known. And if we should meet with Horner,
he would be sure to take acquaintance with us, must wish
her joy, kiss her, talk to her, leer upon her, and the devil
and all. No, I'll not use her to a mask, 'tis dangerous;   100
for masks have made more cuckolds than the best faces that
ever were known.

ALITHEA

How will you do then?

MRS PINCHWIFE

Nay, shall we go? The Exchange will be shut, and I have a
mind to see that.   105

PINCHWIFE

So – I have it – I'll dress her up in the suit we are to carry
down to her brother, little Sir James; nay, I understand
the town tricks. Come, let's go dress her. A mask! No;
a woman masked, like a covered dish, gives a man curiosity
and appetite, when, it may be, uncovered, 'twould turn his   110
stomach; no, no.

ALITHEA

Indeed your comparison is something a greasy one. But
I had a gentle gallant used to say, 'A beauty masked, like the
sun in eclipse, gathers together more gazers than if it
shined out'.   115

Exeunt

---

100 *use* accustom
104 *The Exchange* See II. i.4 and note.
107 *little Sir James* Mrs Pinchwife's brother would have to be small, or the suit would not fit
     Mrs Boutell, who played the part in 1675. The name also suggests that his family are
     country gentry.
112 *greasy* distasteful; with a quibble on the literal sense
113 *like* Q2–5, O (lik'd Q1)

Act III, Scene ii

The scene changes to the New Exchange
[CLASP *and other shopkeepers*]
Enter HORNER, HARCOURT, DORILANT

DORILANT
Engaged to women, and not sup with us?

HORNER
Ay, a pox on 'em all.

HARCOURT
You were much a more reasonable man in the morning,
and had as noble resolutions against 'em as a widower of a
week's liberty.   5

DORILANT
Did I ever think to see you keep company with women
in vain?

HORNER [*Aside*]
In vain! No – 'tis, since I can't love 'em, to be revenged
on 'em.

HARCOURT
Now your sting is gone, you looked in the box, amongst   10
all those women, like a drone in the hive, all upon you;
shoved and ill-used by 'em all, and thrust from one side
to t'other.

DORILANT
Yet he must be buzzing amongst 'em still, like other
old beetle-headed, lickerish drones. Avoid 'em, and hate 'em   15
as they hate you.

HORNER
Because I do hate 'em and would hate 'em yet more,
I'll frequent 'em. You may see by marriage, nothing
makes a man hate a woman more, than her constant
conversation. In short, I converse with 'em, as you do with rich   20
fools, to laugh at 'em and use 'em ill.

Sexist

Trying to keep up front he hates women.

10   *box* i.e., at the theatre
15   *beetle-headed* stupid; *lickerish* greedy, lustful
20   *conversation* intercourse. See I.i. 188.

[93]

DORILANT

But I would no more sup with women, unless I could lie
with 'em, than sup with a rich coxcomb, unless I could
cheat him.

HORNER

Yes, I have known thee sup with a fool for his drinking;   25
if he could set out your hand that way only, you were
satisfied, and if he were a wine-swallowing mouth 'twas
enough.

HARCOURT

Yes, a man drinks often with a fool, as he tosses with a
marker, only to keep his hand in ure. But do the ladies   30
drink?

HORNER

Yes, sir, and I shall have the pleasure at least of laying 'em flat
with a bottle, and bring as much scandal that way upon 'em as
formerly t'other.

HARCOURT

Perhaps you may prove as weak a brother amongst 'em that   35
way as t'other.

DORILANT

Foh! drinking with women is as unnatural as scolding with
'em. But 'tis a pleasure of decayed fornicators, and the basest
way of quenching love.

HARCOURT

Nay, 'tis drowning love instead of quenching it. But leave us for   40
civil women too!

DORILANT

Ay, when he can't be the better for 'em. We hardly pardon
a man that leaves his friend for a wench, and that's a pretty
lawful call.

---

25 *Yes*, Yet (Harold Love, *Yearbook of English Studies*, Vol. 15 (1985), 295.) *Yes* could be spo-
     ken scornfully (Dixon).
26 *set out your hand* serve your purpose, i.e. supply drink. Horner perhaps refers to getting
     free drink, though Harcourt takes him to mean Dorilant will drink with a fool just to
     keep in practice.
29–30 *tosses with a marker, only to keep his hand in ure* throws dice with a scorer, just to keep
     in practice (*OED* Ure *sb.*[1] I.l.a)
35 *brother* member of their fraternity. Harcourt seems to know they are great drinkers.
37–8 *scolding with 'em* joining them in abusive gossip
41 *civil* well-bred

HORNER

Faith, I would not leave you for 'em, if they would not   45
drink.

DORILANT

Who would disappoint his company at Lewis's, for a
gossiping?

HARCOURT

Foh! Wine and women, good apart, together as nauseous
as sack and sugar. But hark you, sir, before you go, a little   50
of your advice; an old maimed general, when unfit for
action, is fittest for counsel. I have other designs upon women
than eating and drinking with them. I am in love with
Sparkish's mistress, whom he is to marry tomorrow. Now how
shall I get her?   55

Enter SPARKISH, *looking about*

HORNER

Why, here comes one will help you to her.

HARCOURT

He! He, I tell you, is my rival, and will hinder my love.

HORNER

No, a foolish rival and a jealous husband assist their
rival's designs; for they are sure to make their women
hate them, which is the first step to their love for another   60
man.

HARCOURT

But I cannot come near his mistress but in his company.

HORNER

Still the better for you, for fools are most easily cheated
when they themselves are accessories; and he is to be
bubbled of his mistress, as of his money, the common mistress,   65
by keeping him company.

SPARKISH

Who is that, that is to be bubbled? Faith, let me snack, I
ha'n't met with a bubble since Christmas. Gad, I think

---

47 *Lewis's* presumably a tavern
50 *sack* Spanish wine, customarily served with sugar. Harcourt's tase is in advance of his
time.
65 *bubbled* tricked
67 *snack* share

bubbles are like their brother woodcocks, go out with the
cold weather.   70

HARCOURT (*Apart to* HORNER)

A pox! he did not hear all I hope.

SPARKISH

Come, you bubbling rogues you, where do we sup? –
Oh, Harcourt, my mistress tells me you have been
making fierce love to her all the play long, ha, ha! – But
I –   75

HARCOURT

I make love to her?

SPARKISH

Nay, I forgive thee; for I think I know thee, and I know her,
but I am sure I know myself.

HARCOURT

Did she tell you so? I see all women are like these of the
Exchange, who, to enhance the price of their commodities,   80
report to their fond customers offers which were never
made 'em.

HORNER

Ay, women are as apt to tell before the intrigue as men
after it, and so show themselves the vainer sex. But hast
thou a mistress, Sparkish? 'Tis as hard for me to believe   85
it as that thou ever hadst a bubble, as you bragged just
now.

SPARKISH

Oh, your servant, sir; are you at your raillery, sir? But we
were some of us beforehand with you today at the play.
The wits were something bold with you, sir; did you not   90
hear us laugh?

HARCOURT

Yes, but I thought you had gone to plays to laugh at the poet's
wit, not at your own.

69 *woodcocks* migratory birds; dupes. Woodcock is the name of a fop in Shadwell's *The
Sullen Lovers* (1668).
   go out disappear
81 *fond* foolish, credulous
88 *your servant* here, a polite form of disagreement
92 sp *HARCOURT Har.* Q1–5, O, but perhaps *Hor.* intended, as Sparkish's speech is addressed
to Horner. However, perhaps Harcourt defends him.

SPARKISH

Your servant, sir; no, I thank you. Gad, I go to a play as to a
country treat. I carry my own wine to one, and my own   95
wit to t'other, or else I'm sure I should not be merry at either.
And the reason why we are so often louder than the players
is because we think we speak more wit, and so become the
poet's rivals in his audience. For to tell you the truth, we
hate the silly rogues; nay, so much that we find fault even   100
with their bawdy upon the stage, whilst we talk nothing else in
the pit as loud.

HORNER

But, why should'st thou hate the silly poets? Thou hast
too much wit to be one, and they, like whores, are only
hated by each other. And thou dost scorn writing, I'm   105
sure.

SPARKISH

Yes, I'd have you to know, I scorn writing. But women,
women, that make men do all foolish things, make 'em
write songs too. Everybody does it. 'Tis even as common
with lovers as playing with fans; and you can no more   110
help rhyming to your Phyllis than drinking to your
Phyllis.

HARCOURT

Nay, poetry in love is no more to be avoided than
jealousy.

DORILANT

But the poets damned your songs, did they?   115

SPARKISH

Damn the poets! They turned 'em into burlesque, as
they call it. That burlesque is a hocus-pocus trick they
have got, which by the virtue of hictius doctius, topsy-turvy,
they make a wise and witty man in the world a fool upon
the stage, you know not how. – And 'tis therefore I hate   120
'em too, for I know not but it may be my own case; for
they'll put a man into a play for looking asquint. Their
predecessors were contented to make serving-men only

---

111 Poets who wrote songs about Phyllis included Rochester, Sedley, and Wycherley himself.
Dorset's 'A Song on Black Bess' (1668) begins: 'Methinks the poor town has been troubled too long / With Phyllis and Chloris in every song' (*Poems*, ed. Brice Harris, p. 91).
118 *hictius doctius* nonsense term used by jugglers

their stage-fools, but these rogues must have gentlemen,
with a pox to 'em, nay knights. And indeed you shall hardly   125
see a fool upon the stage but he's a knight. And to tell you
the truth, they have kept me these six years from being
a knight in earnest, for fear of being knighted in a play, and
dubbed a fool.

DORILANT

Blame 'em not, they must follow their copy, the age.   130

HARCOURT

But why should'st thou be afraid of being in a play, who
expose yourself every day in the playhouses, and as public
places?

HORNER

'Tis but being on the stage, instead of standing on a bench
in the pit.   135

DORILANT

Don't you give money to painters to draw you like? And
are you afraid of your pictures at length in a playhouse,
where all your mistresses may see you?

SPARKISH

A pox! Painters don't draw the smallpox or pimples in one's
face. Come, damn all your silly authors whatever, all books   140
and booksellers, by the world, and all readers, courteous or
uncourteous.

HARCOURT

But, who comes here, Sparkish?

> *Enter* PINCHWIFE *and his wife in man's clothes,*
> ALITHEA, LUCY *her maid*

SPARKISH

Oh hide me! There's my mistress too.

> SPARKISH *hides himself behind* HARCOURT

---

125 *knights* like Sir Martin Mar-all (see I.i. 259 note), Etherege's Sir Oliver Cockwood (*She
    Would if she Could,* 1668), Wycherley's own Sir Simon Addleplot (*Love in a Wood*), and
    many more
132 *as* equally
136 *like* accurately
137 *at length* at full length
141 *courteous* term formerly used by authors in addressing their readers

HARCOURT

  She sees you.   145

SPARKISH

  But I will not see her. 'Tis time to go to Whitehall, and
I must not fail the drawing-room.

HARCOURT

  Pray, first carry me, and reconcile me to her.

SPARKISH

  Another time! Faith, the King will have supped.

HARCOURT

  Not with the worse stomach for thy absence! Thou art   150
one of those fools that think their attendance at the
King's meals as necessary as his physicians', when you
are more troublesome to him than his doctors, or his
dogs.

SPARKISH

  Pshaw! I know my interest, sir. Prithee, hide me.   155

HORNER

  Your servant, Pinchwife. – What, he knows us not!

PINCHWIFE (*To his wife, aside*)

  Come along.

MRS PINCHWIFE

  Pray, have you any ballads? Give me sixpenny worth.

CLASP

  We have no ballads.

MRS PINCHWIFE

  Then give me *Covent Garden Drollery* and a play or two.   160

---

147 *fail* fail to attend
149 *the King will have supped* 'All persons who had been properly introduced might,
without special invitation, go to see [Charles II] dine, sup, dance, and play at hazard'
(Macaulay, *History of England*, ed. C.H. Firth, vol.1, p. 358).
152–4 Charles II 'had not more application to anything, than the preservation of his health'
(Halifax, *Complete Works*, ed. J.P. Kenyon, p. 264). He also 'took delight to have a number of little spaniels follow him, and lie in his bed-chamber, where often-times he suffered
the bitches to puppy and give suck, which rendered it very offensive, and indeed made
the whole Court nasty and stinking' (Evelyn, *Diary*, 6 February 1685).
159 sp *CLASP* not mentioned in the list of 'The Persons'. Friedman suggests the name is an
abbreviation of 'clasp-man', which could have meant a bookseller (*OED* Clasp *sb.* 7).
160 *Covent Garden Drollery* compilation by Alexander Brome of songs, prologues and
epilogues from plays, published 1672

– Oh, here's *Tarugo's Wiles* and *The Slighted Maiden*. I'll have them.

PINCHWIFE (*Apart to her*)

No, plays are not for your reading. Come along; will you discover yourself?

HORNER

Who is that pretty youth with him, Sparkish?   165

SPARKISH

I believe his wife's brother, because he's something like her; but I never saw her but once.

HORNER

Extremely handsome. I have seen a face like it too. Let us follow 'em.

> *Exeunt* PINCHWIFE, MRS PINCHWIFE;
> ALITHEA, LUCY, HORNER, DORILANT *following them*

HARCOURT

Come, Sparkish, your mistress saw you, and will be   170
angry you go not to her. Besides I would fain be reconciled to her, which none but you can do, dear friend.

SPARKISH

Well, that's a better reason, dear friend. I would not go near her now, for hers or my own sake, but I can deny   175
you nothing; for though I have known thee a great while, never go, if I do not love thee as well as a new acquaintance.

HARCOURT

I am obliged to you indeed, dear friend. I would be well with her, only to be well with thee still; for these ties to wives   180
usually dissolve all ties to friends. I would be contented she should enjoy you a-nights, but I would have you to myself a-days, as I have had, dear friend.

SPARKISH

And thou shalt enjoy me a-days, dear, dear friend, never stir; and I'll be divorced from her, sooner than from thee.   185
Come along –

---

161 *Tarugo's Wiles* comedy by Sir Thomas St Serfe, 1668; *The Slighted Maiden* comedy by Sir Robert Stapleton, 1663. Mrs Pinchwife does not know these plays are completely unfashionable.

177 *never go* don't worry. *Never stir* (ll. 184–5) means much the same.

HARCOURT (*Aside*)

So we are hard put to't, when we make our rival our procurer; but neither she nor her brother would let me come near her now. When all's done, a rival is the best cloak to steal to a mistress under, without suspicion; and when we have once got to her as we desire, we throw him off like other cloaks. 190

Exit SPARKISH, *and* HARCOURT *following him*

Re-enter PINCHWIFE, MRS PINCHWIFE *in man's clothes*

PINCHWIFE (*To* ALITHEA [*off-stage*])

Sister, if you will not go, we must leave you. (*Aside*) The fool her gallant and she will muster up all the young saunterers of this place, and they will leave their dear seamstresses to follow us. What a swarm of cuckolds and cuckold-makers are here! – Come, let's be gone, Mistress Margery. 195

MRS PINCHWIFE

Don't you believe that, I ha'n't half my bellyfull of sights yet. 200

PINCHWIFE

Then walk this way.

MRS PINCHWIFE

Lord, what a power of brave signs are here! Stay – the Bull's Head, the Ram's Head, and the Stag's Head! Dear –

PINCHWIFE

Nay, if every husband's proper sign here were visible, they would be all alike. 205

MRS PINCHWIFE

What d'ye mean by that, bud?

PINCHWIFE

'Tis no matter – no matter, bud.

MRS PINCHWIFE

Pray tell me; nay, I will know.

195–6 There were many seamstresses' shops in the New Exchange. Jokes about seamstresses and male customers were as common as those about secretaries and businessmen today.
202 *signs* tradesmen's signs or symbols. See I.i. 260
205 *husband's proper sign* cuckold's horns. Pinchwife is painfully aware that all the signs show horned creatures.

BREACHES SCENE

PINCHWIFE

They would be all bulls', stags', and rams' heads.   210

Exeunt PINCHWIFE, MRS PINCHWIFE

farce

Re-enter SPARKISH, HARCOURT, ALITHEA, LUCY
at t'other door

SPARKISH

Come, dear madam, for my sake you shall be reconciled
to him.

ALITHEA

For your sake I hate him.

HARCOURT

That's something too cruel, madam, to hate me for his
sake.   215

SPARKISH

Ay indeed, madam, too, too cruel to me, to hate my friend
for my sake.

ALITHEA

I hate him because he is your enemy; and you ought to hate
him too, for making love to me, if you love me.

SPARKISH

That's a good one; I, hate a man for loving you! If he did love   220
you, 'tis but what he can't help; and 'tis your fault not his
if he admires you. I, hate a man for being of my opinion? I'll
ne'er do it, by the world.

ALITHEA

Is it for your honour or mine, to suffer a man to make love
to me, who am to marry you tomorrow?   225

SPARKISH

Is it for your honour or mine, to have me jealous? That
he makes love to you is a sign you are handsome; and that
I am not jealous is a sign you are virtuous. That, I think, is for
your honour.

ALITHEA

But 'tis your honour too I am concerned for.   230

HARCOURT

But why, dearest madam, will you be more concerned for his

210   sd *at t'other door* i.e., on the same side of the stage. See Introduction p. 18.

[102]

honour than he is himself? Let his honour alone, for my sake
and his. He, he has no honour –

SPARKISH

How's that?

HARCOURT

But what my dear friend can guard himself.   235

SPARKISH

Oho, that's right again.

HARCOURT

Your care of his honour argues his neglect of it, which is no
honour to my dear friend here; therefore once more, let his
honour go which way it will, dear madam.

SPARKISH

Ay, ay, were it for my honour to marry a woman whose   240
virtue I suspected, and could not trust her in a friend's
hands?

ALITHEA

Are you not afraid to lose me?

HARCOURT

He afraid to lose you, madam! No, no – you may see how the
most estimable and most glorious creature in the world is   245
valued by him. Will you not see it?

SPARKISH

Right, honest Frank, I have that noble value for her that I
cannot be jealous of her.

ALITHEA

You mistake him. He means you care not for me nor who
has me.   250

SPARKISH

Lord, madam, I see you are jealous! Will you wrest a poor
man's meaning from his words?

ALITHEA

You astonish me, sir, with your want of jealousy.

SPARKISH

And you make me giddy, madam, with your jealousy
and fears, and virtue and honour. Gad, I see virtue   255
makes a woman as troublesome as a little reading or
learning.

251 *jealous* impassioned, apprehensive

[103]

ALITHEA
  Monstrous!
LUCY (*Behind*)
  Well, to see what easy husbands these women of quality
  can meet with! A poor chambermaid can never have   260
  such lady-like luck. Besides, he's thrown away upon
  her; she'll make no use of her fortune, her blessing; none to
  a gentleman for a pure cuckold, for it requires good breeding
  to be a cuckold.
ALITHEA
  I tell you then plainly, he pursues me to marry me.   265
SPARKISH
  Pshaw!
HARCOURT
  Come, madam, you see you strive in vain to make him
  jealous of me. My dear friend is the kindest creature in the
  world to me.
SPARKISH
  Poor fellow.   270
HARCOURT
  But his kindness only is not enough for me, without your
  favour. Your good opinion, dear madam, 'tis that must perfect
  my happiness. Good gentleman, he believes all I say; would
  you would do so. Jealous of me! I would not wrong him nor
  you for the world.   275
                    ALITHEA *walks carelessly to and fro*
SPARKISH
  Look you there; hear him, hear him, and do not walk
  away so.
HARCOURT
  I love you, madam, so –
SPARKISH
  How's that! Nay – now you begin to go too far indeed.
HARCOURT
  So much, I confess, I say I love you, that I would not have   280

---

259 *easy* complaisant
262 *she'll make no use of her fortune* i.e., she will not cuckold him
263 *none to* there is nobody like
275 sd *carelessly* unconcernedly

you miserable, and cast yourself away upon so unworthy
and inconsiderable a thing as what you see here.

Clapping his hand on his breast, points at SPARKISH

SPARKISH

No, faith, I believe thou would'st not. Now his meaning
is plain. But I knew before thou would'st not wrong me nor
her.   285

HARCOURT

No, no heavens forbid the glory of her sex should fall so
low as into the embraces of such a contemptible wretch,
the least of mankind – my dear friend here – I injure
him.   *Embracing* SPARKISH

ALITHEA

Very well.   290

SPARKISH

No, no, dear friend, I knew it. Madam, you see he will
rather wrong himself than me, in giving himself such
names.

ALITHEA

Do not you understand him yet?

SPARKISH

Yes, how modestly he speaks of himself, poor fellow.   295

ALITHEA

Methinks he speaks impudently of yourself, since –
before yourself too; insomuch that I can no longer suffer
his scurrilous abusiveness to you, no more than his love to
me.   *Offers to go*

SPARKISH

Nay, nay, madam, pray stay. His love to you! Lord, madam,   300
has he not spoke yet plain enough?

ALITHEA

Yes indeed, I should think so.

288 *least* Q2–5, O (last Q1); 'last' is defensible, but 'least' is clearer.

291 *it. Madam,* Q2 (it Madam, Q1; it, Madam, Q3; it: Madam, Q4–5, O)

296 *since* sir (T.W. Craik, privately). Arguably since is a printer's error and emendation makes
better sense of the dash, but Q1 is defensible; see next note.

296–7 *since – before yourself too* especially since he says it to your face. The dash adds
emphasis (Dixon).

SPARKISH

 Well then, by the world, a man can't speak civilly to a
 woman now but presently she says he makes love to her!
 Nay, madam, you shall stay, with your pardon, since you 305
 have not yet understood him, till he has made an
 éclaircissement of his love to you, that is, what kind of love
 it is. [*To* HARCOURT] Answer to thy catechism: friend, do you
 love my mistress here?

HARCOURT

 Yes, I wish she would not doubt it. 310

SPARKISH

 But how do you love her?

HARCOURT

 With all my soul.

ALITHEA

 I thank him; methinks he speaks plain enough now.

SPARKISH (*To* ALITHEA)

 You are out still. – But with what kind of love,
 Harcourt? 315

HARCOURT

 With the best and truest love in the world.

SPARKISH

 Look you there then, that is with no matrimonial love, I'm
 sure.

ALITHEA

 How's that? Do you say matrimonial love is not best?

SPARKISH [*Aside*]

 Gad, I went too far ere I was aware. – But speak for 320
 thyself, Harcourt; you said you would not wrong me nor
 her.

HARCOURT

 No, no, madam, e'en take him for heaven's sake –

SPARKISH

 Look you there, madam.

---

307 *éclaircissement* elucidation; an affectation
314 *out* mistaken
317 *no matrimonial love* Sparkish falls into the usual cynicism about marriage.
320 sd [*Aside*] But perhaps he is foolish enough to speak openly?

HARCOURT

Who should in all justice be yours, he that loves you   325
most.   *Claps his hand on his breast*

ALITHEA

Look you there, Master Sparkish, who's that?

SPARKISH

Who should it be? – Go on, Harcourt.

HARCOURT

Who loves you more than women titles, or fortune fools.
                                   Points at SPARKISH

SPARKISH

Look you there, he means me still, for he points at me.   330

ALITHEA

Ridiculous!

HARCOURT

Who can only match your faith and constancy in love.

SPARKISH

Ay.

HARCOURT

Who knows, if it be possible, how to value so much beauty
and virtue.   335

SPARKISH

Ay.

HARCOURT

Whose love can no more be equalled in the world than that
heavenly form of yours.

SPARKISH

No.

HARCOURT

Who could no more suffer a rival than your absence, and yet   340
could no more suspect your virtue than his own constancy in
his love to you.

SPARKISH

No.

---

329 *more than women titles, or fortune fools* more than women love titles, or fortune loves fools.
'Fortune favours fools' was proverbial, and is echoed again by Harcourt at ll. 535–6.

HARCOURT

Who, in fine, loves you better than his eyes, that first made
him love you.   345

SPARKISH

Ay – nay, madam, faith, you shan't go, till –

ALITHEA

Have a care, lest you make me stay too long –

SPARKISH

But till he has saluted you; that I may be assured you are
friends, after his honest advice and declaration. Come,
pray, madam, be friends with him.   350

Enter PINCHWIFE, MRS PINCHWIFE

ALITHEA

You must pardon me, sir, that I am not yet so obedient
to you.

PINCHWIFE

What, invite your wife to kiss men? Monstrous! Are you
not ashamed? I will never forgive you.

SPARKISH

Are you not ashamed that I should have more confidence   355
in the chastity of your family than you have? You must not
teach me; I am a man of honour, sir, though I am frank and free.
I am frank, sir –

PINCHWIFE

Very frank, sir, to share your wife with your friends.

SPARKISH

He is an humble, menial friend, such as reconciles the   360
differences of the marriage bed. You know man and wife
do not always agree; I design him for that use, therefore
would have him well with my wife.

---

344 *in fine* finally, in short; French *enfin*. In Dryden's *Sir Martin Mar-all* (1667) Moody, who
      hates fashionable gallicisms, demands an explanation of the phrase, and is told "Tis a
      phrase *à-la-mode*, Sir, and is used in conversation now, as a whiff of tobacco was for-
      merly, in the midst of a discourse, for a thinking while' (III.i.).
348 *saluted* kissed
349 *advice* opinion
358 *frank and free* unconventional; a very vague phrase
359 *frank* generous; sarcastic
360 *menial* family

HORNER (*To* MRS PINCHWIFE)

Had you not rather stay with us? – Prithee, Pinchwife, who is
this pretty young gentleman?   410

PINCHWIFE

One to whom I'm a guardian. (*Aside*) I wish I could keep her
out of your hands.

HORNER

Who is he? I never saw anything so pretty in all my life.

PINCHWIFE

Pshaw! <u>do not look upon him so much; he's a poor bashful
youth, you'll put him out of countenance.</u> Come away,   415
brother.   *Offers to take her away*

HORNER

Oh, your brother?

PINCHWIFE

Yes, my wife's brother. Come, come, she'll stay supper
for us.

HORNER

I thought so, for he is very like her I saw you at the play with, 420
whom I told you I was in love with.

MRS PINCHWIFE (*Aside*)

O Jeminy! Is this he that was in love with me? I am glad on't,
I vow, for he's a curious fine gentleman, and I love him
already too. (*To* PINCHWIFE) Is this he, bud?

PINCHWIFE

Come away, come away!   425

HORNER

Why, what haste are you in? Why won't you let me talk
with him?

PINCHWIFE

Because you'll debauch him. He's yet young and
innocent, and I would not have him debauched for
anything in the world. (*Aside*) How she gazes on him!   430
The devil!

HORNER

Harcourt, Dorilant, look you here; this is the likeness of
that dowdy he told us of, his wife. Did you ever see a lovelier

---

418   *stay* delay
422   *O Jeminy!* corruption of Gemini; expression often used by unsophisticated characters
423   *curious* remarkably
433   *dowdy* unattractive woman

creature? The rogue has reason to be jealous of his wife, since she is like him, for she would make all that see her in love with her. 435

HARCOURT

And as I remember now, she is as like him here as can be.

DORILANT

She is indeed very pretty, if she be like him.

HORNER

Very pretty? A very pretty commendation! She is a glorious creature, beautiful beyond all things I ever beheld. 440

pretty repeated

PINCHWIFE

So, so.

HARCOURT

More beautiful than a poet's first mistress of imagination. 445

HORNER

Or another man's last mistress of flesh and blood.

MRS PINCHWIFE

Nay, now you jeer sir; pray don't jeer me –

PINCHWIFE

Come, come. (*Aside*) By heavens, she'll discover herself.

HORNER

I speak of your sister, sir. 450

PINCHWIFE

Ay, but saying she was handsome, if like him, made him blush. (*Aside*) I am upon a rack!

HORNER

Methinks he is so handsome, he should not be a man.

PINCHWIFE [*Aside*]

Oh, there 'tis out, he has discovered her. I am not able to suffer any longer. (*To his wife*) Come, come away, I say. 455

HORNER

Nay, by your leave, sir, he shall not go yet. (*To them*) Harcourt, Dorilant, let us torment this jealous rogue a little.

447   *jeer* make fun (of)

[112]

HARCOURT *and* DORILANT

    How?   460

HORNER

    I'll show you.

PINCHWIFE

    Come, pray let him go, I cannot stay fooling any longer; I tell
    you his sister stays supper for us.

HORNER

    Does she? Come then, we'll all go sup with her and
    thee.   465

PINCHWIFE

    No, now I think on't, having stayed so long for us, I
    warrant she's gone to bed. *(Aside)* I wish she and I were
    well out of their hands. – Come, I must rise early tomorrow,
    come.

HORNER

    Well then, if she be gone to bed, I wish her and you a   470
    good night. But pray, young gentleman, present my humble
    service to her.

MRS PINCHWIFE

    Thank you heartily, sir.

PINCHWIFE *(Aside)*

    'Sdeath! she will discover herself yet in spite of me. – He is
    something more civil to you, for your kindness to his sister,   475
    than I am, it seems.

HORNER

    Tell her, dear sweet little gentleman, for all your brother there,
    that you have revived the love I had for her at first sight in
    the playhouse.

MRS PINCHWIFE

    But did you love her indeed, and indeed?   480

PINCHWIFE *(Aside)*

    So, so. – Away, I say.

HORNER

    Nay, stay. Yes, indeed, and indeed, pray do you tell her so,
    and give her this kiss from me.   *Kisses her*

PINCHWIFE *(Aside)*

    O heavens! What do I suffer! Now 'tis too plain he knows
    her, and yet –   485

HORNER

    And this, and this –   *Kisses her again*

MRS PINCHWIFE

What do you kiss me for? I am no woman.

PINCHWIFE (*Aside*)

So, there 'tis out. – Come, I cannot, nor will stay any
longer.

HORNER

Nay, they shall send your lady a kiss too. Here Harcourt, Dorilant,   490
will you not?   *They kiss her*

PINCHWIFE (*Aside*)

How! do I suffer this? Was I not accusing another just now
for this rascally patience, in permitting his wife to be kissed
before his face? Ten thousand ulcers gnaw away their lips! Come,
come.   495

HORNER

Good night, dear little gentleman; madam, goodnight;
farewell, Pinchwife. (*Apart to* HARCOURT *and* DORILANT) Did not
I tell you I would raise his jealous gall?

                    Exeunt HORNER, HARCOURT *and* DORILANT

PINCHWIFE

So, they are gone at last! Stay, let me see first if the coach be
at this door.   *Exit*   500

            HORNER, HARCOURT *and* DORILANT *return*

HORNER

What, not gone yet? Will you be sure to do as I desired you,
sweet sir?

MRS PINCHWIFE

Sweet sir, but what will you give me then?

HORNER

Anything. Come away into the next walk.

                    Exit HORNER, *haling away* MRS PINCHWIFE

ALITHEA

Hold, hold! What d'ye do?   505

LUCY

Stay, stay, hold –

HARCOURT

Hold, madam, hold! Let him present him, he'll come

504 *walk* gallery of the New Exchange
      sd *haling* dragging
507 *present him* give him a present

[114]

presently; nay, I will never let you go till you answer my
question.

ALITHEA, LUCY, *struggling with* HARCOURT *and* DORILANT

LUCY

For god's sake, sir, I must follow 'em.   510

DORILANT

No, I have something to present you with too; you shan't
follow them.

PINCHWIFE *returns*

PINCHWIFE

Where? – how? – what's become of? – gone! – whither?

LUCY

He's only gone with the gentleman, who will give him something,
an't please your worship.   515

PINCHWIFE

Something! Give him something, with a pox! – Where are
they?

ALITHEA

In the next walk only, brother.

PINCHWIFE

Only, only! Where, where?

Exit PINCHWIFE *and returns presently, then goes out again*

HARCOURT

What's the matter with him? Why so much concerned? But   520
dearest madam –

ALITHEA

Pray, let me go, sir; I have said and suffered enough
already.

HARCOURT

Then you will not look upon, nor pity, my sufferings?

ALITHEA

To look upon 'em, when I cannot help 'em, were cruelty not   525
pity; therefore I will never see you more.

HARCOURT

Let me then, madam, have my privilege of a banished lover,

508 *presently* immediately
509 *question* that posed at ll. 381–3
515 *an't* if it

[115]

complaining or railing, and giving you but a farewell reason
why, if you cannot condescend to marry me, you should not
take that wretch my rival.   530

ALITHEA

He only, not you, since my honour is engaged so far to
him, can give me a reason, why I should not marry him. But
if he be true, and what I think him to me, I must be so to him.
Your servant, sir.

HARCOURT

Have women only constancy when 'tis a vice, and, like   535
fortune, only true to fools?

DORILANT (*To* LUCY, *who struggles to get from him*)

Thou shalt not stir, thou robust creature! You see I can
deal with you, therefore you should stay the rather, and be
kind.

Enter PINCHWIFE

PINCHWIFE

Gone, gone, not to be found! quite gone! Ten thousand   540
plagues go with 'em! Which way went they?

ALITHEA

But into t'other walk, brother.

LUCY

Their business will be done presently sure, an't please your
worship; it can't be long in doing, I'm sure on't.

ALITHEA

Are they not there?   545

PINCHWIFE

No; you know where they are, you infamous wretch, eternal
shame of your family, which you do not dishonour enough
yourself, you think, but you must help her to do it too, thou legion
of bawds!

ALITHEA

Good brother –   550

PINCHWIFE

Damned, damned sister!

---

535   *like* Q1–3 (are like Q4–5, O)
536   *fortune, only true to fools* See 1. 330 above.
539   *kind* ready for sex; as at V.iv.110
543   *business* For the innuendo, of which Lucy may be innocent, see II.i. 601.

ALITHEA

Look you here, she's coming.

Enter MRS PINCHWIFE *in man's clothes, running,*
with her hat under her arm,
full of oranges and dried fruit; HORNER *following*

MRS PINCHWIFE

O dear bud, look you here what I have got, see.

PINCHWIFE (*Aside, rubbing his forehead*)

And what I have got here too, which you can't see.

MRS PINCHWIFE

The fine gentleman has given me better things yet.   555

PINCHWIFE

Has he so? (*Aside*) Out of breath and coloured! I must hold
yet.

HORNER

I have only given your little brother an orange, sir.

PINCHWIFE (*To* HORNER)

Thank you sir. (*Aside*) You have only squeezed my orange,
I suppose, and given it me again. Yet I must have a city-   560
patience. (*To his wife*) Come, come away.

MRS PINCHWIFE

Stay, till I have put up my fine things, bud.

Enter SIR JASPAR FIDGET

SIR JASPAR

O Master Horner, come, come, the ladies stay for you;
your mistress, my wife, wonders you make not more haste
to her.   565

552 sd *oranges and dried fruit* evidently China (sweet) oranges (IV.ii. 13) and presumably
     Mediterranean dates and figs. An exotic and suggestive gift.
556 *hold* restrain myself
559 *squeezed my orange* debauched my wife. The sexual sense is clear in, for example, John
     Crowne's *The Country Wit* (1676), when Ramble says of his cuckold, 'when I had squeezed
     his orange, I gave him the rind again' (II. iii). Orange wenches in the theatres were often
     prostitutes.
560–1 *city-patience* the patience of a city husband who will not admit he has been cuckolded.
     See I.i. 8 and note.
561–2 Pinchwife remains on stage, but does not hear the references to Horner's supposed
     impotence (ll. 580–9).

HORNER

I have stayed this half hour for you here, and 'tis your fault
I am not now with your wife.

SIR JASPAR

But pray, don't let her know so much. The truth on't
is, I was advancing a certain project to his majesty
about – I'll tell you.   570

HORNER

No, let's go and hear it at your house. Good night, sweet little
gentleman. One kiss more; you'll remember me now, I
hope.   *Kisses her*

DORILANT

What, Sir Jaspar, will you separate friends? He promised to
sup with us, and if you take him to your house, you'll be in   575
danger of our company too.

SIR JASPAR

Alas, gentlemen, my house is not fit for you; there are
none but civil women there, which are not for your turn.
He, you know, can bear with the society of civil women
now, ha, ha, ha! Besides, he's one of my family – he's – he, he,   580
he!

DORILANT

What is he?

SIR JASPAR

Faith, my eunuch, since you'll have it, he, he, he!

[Exeunt] SIR JASPAR FIDGET *and* HORNER

DORILANT

I rather wish thou wert his, or my cuckold. Harcourt, what
a good cuckold is lost there for want of a man to make him   585
one! Thee and I cannot have Horner's privilege, who can make
use of it.

HARCOURT

Ay, to poor Horner 'tis like coming to an estate at three-score,
when a man can't be the better for't.

PINCHWIFE

Come.   590

---

569 *project* an absurd scheme, like those Sir Politick Would-be outlines in *Volpone*
       IV.i. 46–125
579 *civil* respectable. For the innuendo, which does not occur to Sir Jaspar, see I.i. 116–8.
584 *rather wish* wish rather

MRS PINCHWIFE
    Presently, bud.
DORILANT
    Come, let us go too. (*To* ALITHEA) Madam, your servant.
    (*To* LUCY) Good night, strapper.
HARCOURT
    Madam, though you will not let me have a good day, or
    night, I wish you one; but dare not name the other half of   595
    my wish.
ALITHEA
    Good night, sir, for ever.
MRS PINCHWIFE
    I don't know where to put this. Here, dear bud, you
    shall eat it. Nay, you shall have part of the fine gentleman's
    good things, or treat as you call it, when we come   600
    home.
PINCHWIFE
    Indeed, I deserve it, since I furnished the best part of it.
                                        (*Strikes away the orange*)
        The gallant treats, presents, and gives the ball;
        But 'tis the absent cuckold, pays for all.   [*Exeunt*]

Act IV, Scene i

In PINCHWIFE's *house in the morning*
LUCY, ALITHEA *dressed in new clothes*

LUCY
    Well, madam, now have I dressed you, and set you out
    with so many ornaments, and spent upon you ounces of
    essence and pulvilio; and all this for no other purpose
    but as people adorn and perfume a corpse for a stinking
    second-hand grave, such or as bad I think Master Sparkish's   5
    bed.
ALITHEA
    Hold your peace.

---

593   *strapper* strapping (tall and robust) girl

  3   *essence* perfume; *pulvilio* perfumed powder
  5   *second-hand* opened for a second burial (Dixon).

LUCY

Nay, madam, I will ask you the reason why you would banish
poor Master Harcourt for ever from your sight? How could you
be so hard-hearted?   10

ALITHEA

'Twas because I was not hard-hearted.

LUCY

No, no; 'twas stark love and kindness, I warrant.

ALITHEA

It was so. I would see him no more, because I love him.

LUCY

Hey-day, a very pretty reason!

ALITHEA

You do not understand me.   15

LUCY

I wish you may yourself.

ALITHEA

I was engaged to marry, you see, another man, whom my
justice will not suffer me to deceive or injure.

LUCY

Can there be a greater cheat or wrong done to a man than to
give him your person without your heart? I should make a   20
conscience of it.

ALITHEA

I'll retrieve it for him after I am married a while.

LUCY

The woman that marries to love better will be as much
mistaken as the wencher that marries to live better. No,
madam, marrying to increase love is like gaming to   25
become rich; alas, you only lose what little stock you had
before.

ALITHEA

I find by your rhetoric you have been bribed to betray
me.

LUCY

Only by his merit, that has bribed your heart, you see,   30
against your word and rigid honour. But what a devil is
this honour? 'Tis sure a disease in the head, like the

20–1 *make a conscience of it* make it a matter of conscience not to

megrim, or falling sickness, that always hurries people
away to do themselves mischief. Men lose their lives by
it; women what's dearer to 'em, their love, the life of   35
life.

ALITHEA

Come, pray talk you no more of honour, nor Master Harcourt.
I wish the other would come, to secure my fidelity to him and
his right in me.

LUCY

You will marry him then?   40

ALITHEA

Certainly. I have given him already my word, and will my
hand too, to make it good, when he comes.

LUCY

Well, I wish I may never stick pin more if he be not an arrant
natural to t'other fine gentleman.

ALITHEA

I own he wants the wit of Harcourt, which I will dispense   45
withal for another want he has, which is want of jealousy; which
men of wit seldom want.

LUCY

Lord, madam, what should you do with a fool to your
husband? You intend to be honest, don't you? Then
that husbandly virtue, credulity, is thrown away upon   50
you.

ALITHEA

He only that could suspect my virtue should have cause to
do it. 'Tis Sparkish's confidence in my truth that obliges me
to be so faithful to him.

LUCY

You are not sure his opinion may last.   55

ALITHEA

I am satisfied 'tis impossible for him to be jealous, after
the proofs I have had of him. Jealousy in a husband,
heaven defend me from it! It begets a thousand plagues

---

33   *megrim* migraine
     falling sickness epilepsy
43–4 *arrant natural to* obvious born fool compared with
45–6 *dispense withal* do without
49   *honest* chaste

to a poor woman, the loss of her honour, her quiet, and
her –   60

LUCY

And her pleasure.

ALITHEA

What d'ye mean, impertinent?

LUCY

Liberty is a great pleasure, madam.

ALITHEA

I say, loss of her honour, her quiet, nay, her life sometimes;
and what's as bad almost, the loss of this town, that is, she is   65
sent into the country, which is the last ill usage of a husband
to a wife, I think.

LUCY (*Aside*)

Oh, does the wind lie there? – Then of necessity, madam,
you think a man must carry his wife into the country, if he
be wise. The country is as terrible, I find, to our young   70
English ladies as a monastery to those abroad. And on
my virginity, I think they would rather marry a London
jailer than a high sheriff of a county, since neither can
stir from his employment. Formerly women of wit married
fools for a great estate, a fine seat, or the like; but now 'tis   75
for a pretty seat only in Lincoln's Inn Fields, St James's Fields,
or the Pall Mall.

> *Enter to them* SPARKISH, *and* HARCOURT
> *dressed like a parson*

SPARKISH

Madam, your humble servant, a happy day to you, and to
us all.

HARCOURT

Amen.   80

65–7   Similarly Harriet, the heroine of *The Man of Mode,* is so in love with 'this dear town' that
     she 'can scarce endure the country in landscapes and in hangings' (III.i. 92–3). Such views
    ·   would sound less extreme to the original London audience.

70–2   In *L'École des Femmes* (see Introduction, p. 16) Agnes has been not only brought up in
     the country but also educated at a convent.

76–7   *Lincoln's Inn Fields, St James's Fields, or the Pall Mall* fashionable places to live. The earls
     of Bristol and Sandwich lived in Lincoln's Inn Fields, the earls of Clarendon and Oxford
     in St James's Square, which had been laid out in St James's Fields, and Sir William Tem-
     ple, Robert Boyle and Nell Gwyn in Pall Mall.

ALITHEA

Who have we here?

SPARKISH

My chaplain faith. O madam, poor Harcourt remembers his
humble service to you, and in obedience to your last commands,
refrains coming into your sight.

ALITHEA

Is not that he?   85

SPARKISH

No, fie no; but to show that he ne'er intended to hinder
our match, has sent his brother here to join our
hands. When I get me a wife, I must get her a chaplain,
according to the custom. This is his brother, and my
chaplain.   90

ALITHEA

His brother?

LUCY (*Aside*)

And your chaplain, to preach in your pulpit then!

ALITHEA

His brother!

SPARKISH

Nay, I knew you would not believe it. – I told you, sir, she
would take you for your brother Frank   95

ALITHEA

Believe it!

LUCY (*Aside*)

His brother! ha, ha, he! He has a trick left still, it seems.

SPARKISH

Come, my dearest, pray let us go to church before the
canonical hour is past.

ALITHEA

For shame, you are abused still.   100

SPARKISH

By the world, 'tis strange now you are so incredulous.

88–9 It seems Sparkish has engaged Harcourt permanently, as a domestic chaplain. Macaulay
      describes the low status of such chaplains in *The History of England,* ch. 3. Jeremy
      Collier complains of Wycherley's abuse of the clergy here in *A Short View,* p.100; see
      Introduction, pp. 22 and 23

  92 *preach in your pulpit* have sex with you (Farmer and Henley, under 'pulpit'). The aside
      is to Alithea.

98–9 *before the canonical hour is past* before noon. The Anglican Book of Canons allowed
      marriages to be solemnised in church between 8 a.m. and noon. See also ll. 183–5 and note.

ALITHEA

'Tis strange you are so credulous.

SPARKISH

Dearest of my life, hear me. I tell you this is Ned Harcourt
of Cambridge, by the world; you see he has a sneaking college
look. 'Tis true he's something like his brother Frank, and   105
they differ from each other no more than in their age, for they
were twins.

LUCY

Ha, ha, he!

ALITHEA

Your servant, sir; I cannot be so deceived, though you
are. But come, let's hear, how do you know what you affirm   110
so confidently?

SPARKISH

Why, I'll tell you all. Frank Harcourt coming to me this
morning to wish me joy and present his service to you,
I asked him if he could help me to a parson. Whereupon
he told me he had a brother in town who was in orders,   115
and he went straight away and sent him you see there, to
me.

ALITHEA

Yes, Frank goes and puts on a black coat, then tells you he is
Ned. That's all you have for't!

SPARKISH

Pshaw, pshaw! I tell you by the same token, the midwife   120
put her garter about Frank's neck to know 'em asunder, they
were so like.

ALITHEA

Frank tells you this too?

SPARKISH

Ay, and Ned there too. Nay, they are both in a story.

ALITHEA

So, so; very foolish.   125

---

104 *Cambridge* The clergy were educated at Oxford and Cambridge.
104–5 *sneaking college look* OED sneaking *a.* 2 quotes J. Beaumont, *Psyche*(1648): 'No conven-
ticle's sneaking cloisters hid those doctrines'. In Thomas Shadwell's *The Humourists* (1670)
Sneak, a domestic chaplain, is also 'a fellow of a college' (*dramatis personae*).
124 *in a story* tell the same story

SPARKISH

Lord, if you won't believe one, you had best try him by your chambermaid there; for chambermaids must needs know chaplains from other men, they are so used to 'em.

LUCY

Let's see; nay, I'll be sworn he has the canonical smirk, and   130 the filthy, clammy palm of a chaplain.

ALITHEA

Well, most reverend doctor, pray let us make an end of this fooling.

HARCOURT

With all my soul, divine, heavenly creature, when you please.   135

ALITHEA

He speaks like a chaplain indeed.

SPARKISH

Why, was there not 'soul', 'divine', 'heavenly' in what he said?

ALITHEA

Once more, most impertinent black coat, cease your persecution, and let us have a conclusion of this ridiculous   140 love.

HARCOURT (*Aside*)

I had forgot – I must suit my style to my coat, or I wear it in vain.

ALITHEA

I have no more patience left. Let us make once an end of this troublesome love, I say.   145

HARCOURT

So be it, seraphic lady, when your honour shall think it meet and convenient so to do.

127–9 Macaulay says 'the relation between divines and handmaidens was a theme for endless jest' (*History of England,* ch. 3); Hunt quotes John Phillips, 'There sits a chamber maid upon a hassock / Whom th' chaplain oft instructs without his cassock' (*Satyr against Hypocrites,* 1655). But Lucy's comments, especially at ll. 162–3, suggest there was some truth in such allegations.

144 *once* once for all

147 *so to do* Harcourt suits his style to his coat and echoes the communion service in the *Book of Common Prayer.* 'It is meet and right so to do'. Not being a genuine clergyman, he echoes the congregation's response.

SPARKISH

Gad, I'm sure none but a chaplain could speak so, I think.

ALITHEA

Let me tell you sir, this dull trick will not serve your turn. Though you delay our marriage, you shall not hinder it. 150

HARCOURT

Far be it from me, munificent patroness, to delay your marriage. I desire nothing more than to marry you presently, which I might do, if you yourself would; for my noble, 155 good-natured and thrice generous patron here would not hinder it.

SPARKISH

No, poor man, not I, faith.

HARCOURT

And now, madam, let me tell you plainly, nobody else shall marry you. By heavens, I'll die first, for I'm sure I should die 160 after it.

LUCY [*Aside*]

How his love has made him forget his function, as I have seen it in real parsons!

ALITHEA

That was spoken like a chaplain too! Now you understand him, I hope. 165

SPARKISH

Poor man, he takes it heinously to be refused. I can't blame him, 'tis putting an indignity upon him not to be suffered. But you'll pardon me, madam, it shan't be; he shall marry us. Come away, pray, madam.

LUCY [*Aside*]

Ha, ha, he! More ado! 'Tis late. 170

ALITHEA

Invincible stupidity! I tell you he would marry me as your rival, not as your chaplain.

SPARKISH (*Pulling her away*)

Come, come, madam.

160–1 *die after it* possibly, have orgasm after marriage. This was a common meaning of 'die' at the time, though the standard meaning is clearer.
  166 *takes it heinously* is grievously offended

LUCY

I pray, madam, do not refuse this reverend divine the honour
and satisfaction of marrying you; for I dare say he has set his   175
heart upon't, good doctor.

ALITHEA [*To* HARCOURT]

What can you hope or design by this?

HARCOURT [*Aside*]

I could answer her, a reprieve for a day only often revokes
a hasty doom. At worst, if she will not take mercy on me
and let me marry her, I have at least the lover's second   180
pleasure, hindering my rival's enjoyment, though but for
a time.

SPARKISH

Come, madam, 'tis e'en twelve o'clock, and my mother
charged me never to be married out of the canonical hours.
Come, come! Lord, here's such a deal of modesty, I warrant, the   185
first day.

LUCY

Yes, an't please your worship, married women show all their
modesty the first day, because married men show all their love the
first day.

Exeunt SPARKISH, ALITHEA, HARCOURT *and* LUCY

Act IV, Scene ii

The scene changes to a bedchamber,
where appear PINCHWIFE, MRS PINCHWIFE

PINCHWIFE

Come, tell me, I say.

MRS PINCHWIFE

Lord! ha'n't I told it an hundred times over?

PINCHWIFE (*Aside*)

I would try if, in the repetition of the ungrateful tale, I
could find her altering it in the least circumstance; for

---

183   *e'en* almost. Normally in such a phrase the meaning would be 'precisely', but Sparkish
does not seem to think he has missed the canonical hours.

183–4   *my mother charged me* perhaps a characteristic foppish expression; also used by Sir Simon
Addleplot, *Love in a Wood* I.ii. 203

3   *ungrateful* disagreeable

[127]

if her story be false, she is so too. – Come, how was't,   5
baggage?

MRS PINCHWIFE

Lord, what pleasure you take to hear it, sure!

PINCHWIFE

No, you take more in telling it, I find. But speak – how
was't?

MRS PINCHWIFE

He carried me up into the house next to the Exchange.   10

PINCHWIFE

So, and you two were only in the room.

MRS PINCHWIFE

Yes, for he sent away a youth, that was there, for some dried
fruit and China oranges.

PINCHWIFE

Did he so? Damn him for it – and for –

MRS PINCHWIFE

But presently came up the gentlewoman of the house.   15

PINCHWIFE

Oh, 'twas well she did! But what did he do whilst the fruit
came?

MRS PINCHWIFE

He kissed me an hundred times, and told me he fancied he
kissed my fine sister, meaning me, you know, whom he
said he loved with all his soul, and bid me be sure to tell   20
her so, and to desire her to be at her window by eleven of
the clock this morning, and he would walk under it at that
time.

PINCHWIFE (*Aside*)

And he was as good as his word, very punctual, a pox reward
him for't.   25

MRS PINCHWIFE

Well, and he said if you were not within, he would come up
to her, meaning me, you know bud, still.

PINCHWIFE (*Aside*)

So – he knew her certainly. But for this confession I am

10 *house* public house
11 *you two were only* only you two were
13 *China oranges* sweet oranges; a delicacy. The phrase links the bawdy associations of
    oranges (III.ii. 559–60 and note) and China (IV.iii. 84 and note)
16 *whilst* until

[128]

obliged to her simplicity. – But what, you stood very still when he
kissed you?   30

MRS PINCHWIFE

Yes, I warrant you; would you have had me discovered
myself?

PINCHWIFE

But you told me he did some beastliness to you, as you called
it. What was't?

MRS PINCHWIFE

Why, he put –   35

PINCHWIFE

What?

MRS PINCHWIFE

Why, he put the tip of his tongue between my lips, and so
muzzled me – and I said, I'd bite it.

PINCHWIFE

An eternal canker seize it, for a dog!

MRS PINCHWIFE

Nay, you need not be so angry with him neither, for to say   40
truth he has the sweetest breath I ever knew.

PINCHWIFE

The devil! You were satisfied with it then, and would do
it again?

MRS PINCHWIFE

Not unless he should force me.

PINCHWIFE

Force you, changeling! I tell you no woman can be   45
forced.

MRS PINCHWIFE

Yes, but she may sure by such a one as he, for he's a proper,
goodly strong man; 'tis hard, let me tell you, to resist
him.

PINCHWIFE [*Aside*]

So, 'tis plain she loves him, yet she has not love enough   50
to make her conceal it from me. But the sight of him
will increase her aversion for me, and love for him; and
that love instruct her how to deceive me and satisfy him,
all idiot as she is. Love! 'Twas he gave women first their craft,

38   *muzzled* kissed closely; 'a low word' (Johnson)
39   *for a dog* for behaving like a dog
45   *changeling* simpleton

[129]

their art of deluding. Out of nature's hands they came plain,   55
open, silly, and fit for slaves, as she and heaven intended
'em, but damned Love – well – I must strangle that little
monster whilst I can deal with him. – Go fetch pen, ink, and
paper out of the next room.

MRS PINCHWIFE

Yes, bud.   *Exit* MRS PINCHWIFE   60

PINCHWIFE (*Aside*)

Why should women have more invention in love than
men? It can only be because they have more desires,
more soliciting passions, more lust, and more of the
devil.

MRS PINCHWIFE *returns*

Come, minx, sit down and write.   65

MRS PINCHWIFE

Ay, dear bud, but I can't do't very well.

PINCHWIFE

I wish you could not at all.

MRS PINCHWIFE

But what should I write for?

PINCHWIFE

I'll have you write a letter to your lover.

MRS PINCHWIFE

O Lord, to the fine gentleman a letter!   70

PINCHWIFE

Yes, to the fine gentleman.

MRS PINCHWIFE

Lord, you do but jeer; sure you jest.

PINCHWIFE

I am not so merry, come, write as I bid you.

MRS PINCHWIFE

What, do you think I am a fool?

PINCHWIFE [*Aside*]

She's afraid I would not dictate any love to him, therefore   75
she's unwilling. – But you had best begin.

55–6 *plain, open* straightforward, without guile
57–8 *little monster* Cupid
  61 *invention* inventiveness
  63 *soliciting* urgent

MRS PINCHWIFE

    Indeed, and indeed, but I won't, so I won't!

PINCHWIFE

    Why?

MRS PINCHWIFE

    Because he's in town. You may send for him if you will.

PINCHWIFE

    Very well, you would have him brought to you; is   80
    it come to this? I say, take the pen and write, or you'll
    provoke me.

MRS PINCHWIFE

    Lord, what d'ye make a fool of me for? Don't I know that
    letters are never writ but from the country to London
    and from London into the country? Now, he's in town   85
    and I am in town too; therefore I can't write to him, you
    know.

PINCHWIFE (*Aside*)

    So, I am glad it is no worse; she is innocent enough yet. – Yes,
    you may, when your husband bids you, write letters to people
    that are in town.   90

MRS PINCHWIFE

    Oh, may I so? Then I'm satisfied.

PINCHWIFE

    Come, begin. (*Dictates*') 'Sir' –

MRS PINCHWIFE

    Shan't I say 'Dear Sir'? You know one says always something
    more than bare 'Sir'.

PINCHWIFE

    Write as I bid you, or I will write 'whore' with this penknife   95
    in your face.

MRS PINCHWIFE

    Nay, good bud. (*She writes*) 'Sir'.

PINCHWIFE

    'Though I suffered last night your nauseous, loathed kisses
    and embraces' – Write.

---

77 *so I won't* so there; childish expression
94 *bare* merely. But perhaps the word provokes Pinchwife.
95–6 Possibly echoes Othello: 'Was this fair paper, this most goodly book, / Made to write
    "whore" upon?' (*Othello* IV.ii. 73–4).

MRS PINCHWIFE

Nay, why should I say so? You know I told you he had a   100
sweet breath.

PINCHWIFE

Write!

MRS PINCHWIFE

Let me but put out 'loathed'.

PINCHWIFE

Write, I say.

MRS PINCHWIFE

Well, then. (*Writes*)   105

PINCHWIFE

Let's see what you have writ. (*Takes the paper and reads*)
'Though I suffered last night your kisses and embraces'. –
Thou impudent creature! Where is 'nauseous' and
'loathed'?

MRS PINCHWIFE

I can't abide to write such filthy words.   110

PINCHWIFE

Once more write as I'd have you, and question it not, or I
will spoil thy writing with this. (*Holds up the penknife*) I
will stab out those eyes that cause my mischief.

MRS PINCHWIFE

O Lord, I will!

PINCHWIFE

So – so – Let's see now! (*Reads*) 'Though I suffered last night   115
your nauseous, loathed kisses and embraces'. – Go on – 'Yet
I would not have you presume that you shall ever repeat
them'. – So –

MRS PINCHWIFE (*She writes*)

I have writ it.

PINCHWIFE

On then. – 'I then concealed myself from your knowledge, to   120
avoid your insolencies' –

MRS PINCHWIFE (*She writes*)

So –

PINCHWIFE

'The same reason, now I am out of your hands' –

MRS PINCHWIFE (*She writes*)

So –

103   *put out* cross out

[132]

PINCHWIFE

'Makes me own to you my unfortunate, though innocent   125
frolic, of being in man's clothes' –

MRS PINCHWIFE (*She writes*)

So –

PINCHWIFE

'that you may for ever more cease to pursue her, who hates
and detests you' –

MRS PINCHWIFE (*She writes on. Sighs*)

Soh –   130

PINCHWIFE

What, do you sigh? – 'detests you – as much as she loves her
husband and her honour'.

MRS PINCHWIFE

I vow, husband, he'll ne'er believe I should write such a
letter.

PINCHWIFE

What, he'd expect a kinder from you? Come now, your name   135
only.

MRS PINCHWIFE

What, shan't I say 'Your most faithful, humble servant till
death'?

PINCHWIFE

No, tormenting fiend! (*Aside*) Her style, I find, would be
very soft. – Come, wrap it up now, whilst I go fetch   140
wax and a candle, and write on the back side 'For Master
Horner'.   *Exit* PINCHWIFE

MRS PINCHWIFE

'For Master Horner' – So I am glad he has told me his
name. Dear Master Horner! But why should I send thee
such a letter that will vex thee and make thee angry   145
with me? – Well, I will not send it. – Ay, but then my
husband will kill me – for I see plainly, he won't let me
love Master Horner – but what care I for my husband? –
I won't, so I won't send poor Master Horner such a letter–
but then my husband – But oh, what if I writ at   150

135 *kinder* more loving
139 *style* formal conclusion
140 *soft* mollifying

bottom, my husband made me write it? – Ay, but then my
husband would see't – Can one have no shift? Ah, a London
woman would have had a hundred presently. Stay – what if
I should write a letter, and wrap it up like this, and write
upon't too? Ay, but then my husband would see't – I don't   155
know what to do – But yet i'vads I'll try, so I will –
for I will not send this letter to poor Master Horner, come
what will on't.

        (*She writes, and repeats what she hath writ*)
'Dear Sweet Master Horner' – so – 'My husband would
have me send you a base, rude, unmannerly letter – but   160
I won't' – so – 'and would have me forbid you loving me
but I won't' – so – 'and would have me say to you, I
hate you poor Master Horner – but I won't tell a lie for
him' – there – 'for I'm sure if you and I were in the
country at cards together' – so – 'I could not help   165
treading on your toe under the table' – so – 'or rubbing
knees with you, and staring in your face till you saw
me' – very well – 'and then looking down and blushing for an
hour together' – so – 'but I must make haste before my
husband come; and now he has taught me to write   170
letters, you shall have longer ones from me, who am,
dear, dear, poor dear Master Horner, your most humble
friend, and servant to command till death, Margery
Pinchwife'. – Stay, I must give him a hint at bottom – so –
now wrap it up just like t'other – so – now write 'For Master   175
Horner'. – But, oh now, what shall I do with it? For here
comes my husband.

        Enter PINCHWIFE

PINCHWIFE (*Aside*)
    I have been detained by a sparkish coxcomb, who pretended
    a visit to me; but I fear 'twas to my wife. –What, have you
    done?   180
MRS PINCHWIFE
    Ay, ay, bud, just now.

---

152   *shift* expedient
156   *i'vads* in faith; rustic oath
174   *hint at bottom* i.e., the postscript read by Horner at IV.iii. 286–9
178   *sparkish coxcomb* fop, like Sparkish himself. See note to 'The Persons', p. 4.

PINCHWIFE

Let's see't. What d'ye tremble for? What, you would not have it go?

MRS PINCHWIFE

Here. (*Aside*) No, I must not give him that. (*He opens and reads the first letter*) So I had been served if I had ill given him this. 185

PINCHWIFE

Come, where's the wax and seal!

MRS PINCHWIFE (*Aside*)

Lord, what shall I do now? Nay, then, I have it. – Pray, let me see't. Lord, you think me so arrant a fool I cannot seal a letter? I will do't, so I will. 190

> *Snatches the letter from him, changes it for the other, seals it, and delivers it to him*

PINCHWIFE

Nay, I believe you will learn that, and other things too, which I would not have you.

MRS PINCHWIFE

So. Ha'n't I done it curiously? (*Aside*) I think I have; there's my letter going to Master Horner, since he'll needs have me send letters to folks. 195

PINCHWIFE

'Tis very well; but I warrant, you would not have it go now?

MRS PINCHWIFE

Yes, indeed, but I would, bud, now.

PINCHWIFE

Well you are a good girl then. Come, let me lock you up in your chamber till I come back. And be sure you come not 200 within three strides of the window when I am gone, for I have a spy in the street.

> *Exit* MRS PINCHWIFE; PINCHWIFE *locks the door*

At least, 'tis fit she think so. If we do not cheat women, they'll cheat us; and fraud may be justly used with secret enemies,

---

184 *that* i.e., the second letter. She almost hands him the wrong one.
185–6 That is what would have happened if I had given him the second letter, i.e., he would have read it.
193 *curiously* carefully

of which a wife is the most dangerous. And he that has   205
a handsome one to keep, and a frontier town, must
provide against treachery rather than open force. Now I have
secured all within I'll deal with the foe without with false
intelligence.

Holds up the letter
Exit PINCHWIFE

Act IV, Scene iii

The scene changes to HORNER's *lodging*
QUACK *and* HORNER

QUACK
Well, sir, how fadges the new design? Have you not the
luck of all your brother projectors, to deceive only yourself
at last?

HORNER
No, good domine doctor, I deceive you, it seems, and
others too, for the grave matrons and old rigid husbands   5
think me as unfit for love as they are. But their wives,
sisters and daughters know some of 'em better things
already.

QUACK
Already!

HORNER
Already, I say. Last night I was drunk with half a dozen of   10
your civil persons, as you call 'em, and people of honour,
and so was made free of their society and dressing rooms
for ever hereafter; and am already come to the privileges
of sleeping upon their pallets, warming smocks, tying
shoes and garters, and the like, doctor, already, already,   15
doctor.

205–6 *and* and she; *frontier town*, i.e. likely to fall by treachery
208–9 *false intelligence* disinformation

  1 *fadges* gets on
  2 *projectors* schemers. Sir Jaspar, for example, has boasted of 'a certain project' of his
    (III.ii. 570), presumably a crazy scheme.
  4 *domine* master; polite address to a member of a learned profession, here used
    ironically
 14 *pallets* straw mattresses or inferior beds

QUACK

You have made use of your time, sir.

HORNER

I tell thee, I am now no more interruption to 'em when they
sing or talk bawdy than a little squab French page who speaks
no English.   20

QUACK

But do civil persons and women of honour drink and sing
bawdy songs?

HORNER

Oh, amongst friends, amongst friends. For your bigots
in honour are just like those in religion. They fear the
eye of the world more than the eye of heaven, and think   25
there is no virtue but railing at vice, and no sin but giving
scandal. They rail at a poor, little, kept player, and keep
themselves some young, modest pulpit comedian to be
privy to their sins in their closets, not to tell 'em of them in
their chapels.   30

QUACK

Nay, the truth on't is, priests amongst the women now have
quite got the better of us lay confessors, physicians.

HORNER

And they are rather their patients, but –

Enter my LADY FIDGET, *looking about her*

Now we talk of women of honour, here comes one. Step
behind the screen there, and but observe if I have not   35
particular privileges with the women of reputation already,
doctor, already.   [QUACK *steps behind screen*]

LADY FIDGET

Well, Horner, am not I a woman of honour? You see, I'm as
good as my word.

HORNER

And you shall see, madam, I'll not be behindhand with you   40
in honour. And I'll be as good as my word too, if you please
but to withdraw into the next room.

---

19   *squab* chubby; perhaps also shy (Dixon)
27   *kept player* See II.i. 360–5 and notes.
28   *pulpit comedian* domestic chaplain. See IV.i. 88–92 and notes.

LADY FIDGET

But first, my dear sir, you must promise to have a care of my dear honour.

HORNER

If you talk a word more of your honour, you'll make me 45
incapable to wrong it. To talk of honour in the mysteries of
love is like talking of heaven or the deity in an operation of
witchcraft, just when you are employing the devil; it makes the
charm impotent.

LADY FIDGET

Nay, fie, let us not be smutty. But you talk of mysteries and 50
bewitching to me; I don't understand you.

HORNER

I tell you, madam, the word 'money' in a mistress's mouth,
at such a nick of time, is not a more disheartening sound
to a younger brother than that of honour to an eager lover
like myself. 55

LADY FIDGET

But you can't blame a lady of my reputation to be chary.

HORNER

Chary! I have been chary of it already, by the report I have
caused of myself.

LADY FIDGET

Ay, but if you should ever let other women know that dear
secret, it would come out. Nay, you must have a great care 60
of your conduct, for my acquaintance are so censorious – oh
'tis a wicked censorious world, Master Horner! – I say, are
so censorious and detracting that perhaps they'll talk to the
prejudice of my honour, though you should not let them know
the dear secret. 65

HORNER

Nay, madam, rather than they shall prejudice your honour, I'll
prejudice theirs; and to serve you, I'll lie with 'em all, make the
secret their own, and then they'll keep it: I am a Machiavel in love,
madam.

LADY FIDGET

Oh no, sir, not that way. 70

---

54 *younger brother* traditionally short of money, since elder brothers inherited
68 *Machiavel* Machiavellian, unscrupulous plotter

HORNER

Nay, the devil take me, if censorious women are to be silenced any other way!

LADY FIDGET

A secret is better kept, I hope, by a single person than a multitude. Therefore pray do not trust anybody else with it, dear, dear Master Horner.   *(Embracing him)*   75

Enter SIR JASPAR FIDGET

SIR JASPAR

How now!

LADY FIDGET (*Aside*)

O my husband! – prevented! – and what's almost as bad, found with my arms about another man – that will appear too much – what shall I say? – Sir Jaspar, come hither. I am trying if Master Horner were ticklish, and he's as ticklish   80 as can be. I love to torment the confounded toad. Let you and I tickle him.

SIR JASPAR

No, your ladyship will tickle him better without me, I suppose. But is this your buying china? I thought you had been at the china house?   85

HORNER (*Aside*)

China house! That's my cue, I must take it. – A pox! Can't you keep your impertinent wives at home? Some men are troubled with the husbands, but I with the wives. But I'd have you to know, since I cannot be your journeyman by night, I will not be your drudge by day, to squire your   90 wife about and be your man of straw, or scarecrow, only to pies and jays that would be nibbling at your forbidden

---

75 sd *Embracing him* Q1–3 (*omitted*, Q4–5, O). Perhaps in later productions the scene was played in a less sexy manner; see Introduction, p. 23.

84 *buying china* Collecting china was fashionable, but an association between china, Horner, and sex, first hinted at IV.ii. 13, develops from here to l. 204 below. China was usually associated with women and virginity; see Aubrey Williams, 'The "Fall" of China and *The Rape of the Lock*', *Philological Quarterly*, vol. 41 (1962), 412–25, reprinted in *The Rape of the Lock, A Selection of Critical Essays*, ed. John Dixon Hunt (1968).

85 *china house* china shop. A likely place for an assignation – see V.iv. 145–6– though the thought does not strike Sir Jaspar.

89 *journeyman* hireling. The term often had sexual connotations, as here. *drudge* hard worker; another term with sexual connotations. See Shakespeare, Sonnet 151, for an especially clear example.

92 *pies* magpies; pies *and jays* fops

fruit. I shall be shortly the hackney gentleman-usher of
the town.

SIR JASPAR (*Aside*)

He, he, he! Poor fellow, he's in the right on't, faith! To   95
squire women about for other folks is as ungrateful an
employment as to tell money for other folks. – He, he, he!
Ben't angry, Horner.

LADY FIDGET

No, 'tis I have more reason to be angry, who am left by
you to go abroad indecently alone; or, what is more indecent,   100
to pin myself upon such ill-bred people of your acquaintance
as this is.

SIR JASPAR

Nay, prithee, what has he done?

LADY FIDGET

Nay, he has done nothing.

SIR JASPAR

But what d'ye take ill, if he has done nothing?   105

LADY FIDGET

Ha, ha, ha! Faith, I can't but laugh, however. Why, d'ye
think the unmannerly toad would come down to me to
the coach? I was fain to come up to fetch him, or go without
him, which I was resolved not to do; for he knows china very
well, and has himself very good, but will not let me see it   110
lest I should beg some. But I will find it out, and have what I
came for yet.   *Exit* LADY FIDGET *and locks the door,*
                       followed by HORNER *to the door*

HORNER (*Apart to* LADY FIDGET)

Lock the door, madam. – So, she has got into my chamber
and locked me out. Oh, the impertinency of womankind!

---

93 *hackney* hired
    gentleman-usher See II.i. 499 note.
96 *ungrateful* thankless. This echoes Pinchwife, IV.ii. 3.
97 *tell* count
100 *indecently* unbecomingly
104, 105 *nothing* word with bawdy associations unknown to Sir Jaspar. For instance in
    Hamlet 'nothing' is 'a fair thought to lie between maids' legs' (III.ii. 112–13)
107–8 *would come down to me to the coach?* Q5 (would not come down to me to the coach, O).
    Rhetorical question.

Well, Sir Jaspar, plain dealing is a jewel. I₁
your wife to trouble me again here, she shall c₂
a pair of horns, by my Lord Mayor she shall.
cannot furnish you myself, you are sure, yet
a way.

SIR JASPAR (*Aside*)

Ha, ha, he! At my first coming in and finding her arms abou
him, tickling him it seems, I was half jealous, but now I see
my folly. – He, he, he! Poor Horner.

HORNER [*Aside*]

Nay, though you laugh now, 'twill be my turn ere long. –
Oh, women, more impertinent, more cunning and more
mischievous than their monkeys, and to me almost as   125
ugly! Now is she throwing my things about, and rifling
all I have, but I'll get into her the back way, and so rifle her
for it.

SIR JASPAR

Ha, ha, ha! Poor angry Horner.

HORNER

Stay here a little, I'll ferret her out to you presently, I   130
warrant.   *Exit* HORNER *at t'other door.*

SIR JASPAR

Wife! My Lady Fidget! Wife! He is coming into you the back
way!   SIR JASPAR *calls through the door to his wife;*
                                        she answers from within

LADY FIDGET

Let him come, and welcome, which way he will.

SIR JASPAR

He'll catch you, and use you roughly, and be too strong for   135
you.

---

115 *plain dealing is a jewel* proverbial. On the evidence of *The Plain Dealer* it may be doubted
      if Wycherley himself wholly accepted the idea.
125 *monkeys* fashionable pets
127 *the back way* perhaps already a *double entendre* referring to anal intercourse, as in
      ll. 132–4. See note on l. 128 and Richard Levin, *Notes and Queries*, vol. 208 (1963), 338–40
      and 428–9. Levin does not mention Wycherley's likely source in *Volpone* II.vi. 58–61.
      rifle double entendre: 'to coit with, or to caress sexually, a woman' (Partridge)
130 *ferret her out* get her out as a ferret does, by going in at one hole so that the creature
      comes out at another; probably with bawdy associations, as in Shakespeare's *Henry
      V:* ' I'll . . . firk him, and ferret him' (IV.iv. 27–8)
132–4 See l. 127, note.

FIDGET
Don't you trouble yourself, let him if he can.

QUACK (*Behind*)
This indeed I could not have believed from him, nor any but my own eyes.

Enter Mrs SQUEAMISH

SQUEAMISH
Where's this woman-hater, this toad, this ugly, greasy, dirty   140
sloven?

SIR JASPAR [*Aside*]
So the women all will have him ugly. Methinks he is a comely person, but his wants make his form contemptible to 'em; and 'tis e'en as my wife said yesterday, talking of him, that a proper handsome eunuch was as ridiculous a thing as a gigantic   145
coward.

SQUEAMISH
Sir Jaspar, your servant. Where is the odious beast?

SIR JASPAR
He's within in his chamber, with my wife; she's playing the wag with him.

SQUEAMISH
Is she so? And he's a clownish beast, he'll give her   150
no quarter, he'll play the wag with her again, let me tell you. Come, let's go help her. – What, the door's locked?

SIR JASPAR
Ay, my wife locked it.

SQUEAMISH
Did she so? Let us break it open then.   155

SIR JASPAR
No, no, he'll do her no hurt.

SQUEAMISH
No. (*Aside*) But is there no other way to get into 'em? Whither goes this? I will disturb 'em.

Exit SQUEAMISH *at another door*

148–9 *playing the wag* being amusingly mischievous, and/or having sex. See Partridge, *Shakespeare's Bawdy*, under 'wag'. As he was at I.i. 73 Sir Jaspar is innocent of any bawdy meaning, but Mrs Squeamish's repetition of the phrase at l. 151 suggests that her understanding is not altogether literal, contrary to what Horner says at l. 62–3.

Enter OLD LADY SQUEAMISH

OLD LADY SQUEAMISH

Where is this harlotry, this impudent baggage, this rambling
tomrig? O Sir Jaspar, I'm glad to see you here. Did   160
you not see my vild grandchild come in hither just
now?

SIR JASPAR

Yes.

OLD LADY SQUEAMISH

Ay, but where is she then? where is she? Lord, Sir Jaspar, I
have e'en rattled myself to pieces in pursuit of her. But can   165
you tell what she makes here? They say below, no woman
lodges here.

SIR JASPAR

No.

OLD LADY SQUEAMISH

No! What does she here then? Say, if it be not a woman's
lodging, what makes she here? But are you sure no woman   170
lodges here?

SIR JASPAR

No, nor no man neither, this is Master Horner's lodging.

OLD LADY SQUEAMISH

Is it so, are you sure?

SIR JASPAR

Yes, yes.

OLD LADY SQUEAMISH

So – then there's no hurt in't, I hope. But where is he?   175

SIR JASPAR

He's in the next room with my wife.

OLD LADY SQUEAMISH

Nay, if you trust him with your wife, I may with my Biddy.
They say he's a merry harmless man now, e'en as harmless
a man as ever came out of Italy with a good voice, and

---

159   *harlotry* harlot; vaguely abusive
160   *rambling* See II.i. 399 note.
      tomrig bold or immodest woman (*OED*, tomboy, 2)
161   *vild* ed. (vil'd Q1–5, O) vile, depraved (*OED*). I have retained the archaic form, as suited
      to Old Lady Squeamish.
166   *what she makes* what she is doing
177   *Biddy* young woman (Partridge); or abbreviation of Bridget
178–79   *as harmless . . . good voice* as harmless as a castrato. These singers were very fashionable.

as pretty harmless company for a lady as a snake without   180
his teeth.

SIR JASPAR

Ay, ay, poor man.

Enter Mrs SQUEAMISH

SQUEAMISH

I can't find 'em. – Oh, are you here, grandmother? I
followed, you must know, my Lady Fidget hither. 'Tis the
prettiest lodging, and I have been staring on the prettiest   185
pictures.

Enter LADY FIDGET *with a piece of china in her hand,*
and HORNER *following*

LADY FIDGET

And I have been toiling and moiling for the prettiest piece
of china, my dear.

HORNER

Nay, she has been too hard for me, do what I could.

SQUEAMISH

O Lord, I'll have some china too. Good Master Horner, don't   190
think to give other people china, and me none. Come in with
me too.

HORNER

Upon my honour I have none left now.

SQUEAMISH

Nay, nay, I have known you deny your china before now, but
you shan't put me off so. Come.   195

HORNER

This lady had the last there.

LADY FIDGET

Yes indeed, madam, to my certain knowledge he has no more
left.

SQUEAMISH

Oh, but it may be he may have some you could not find.

LADY FIDGET

What, d'ye think if he had had any left, I would not have   200

186   *pictures* perhaps pornographic. See I.i. 79 and note.
187   *toiling and moiling* working hard

had it too? For we women of quality never think we have
china enough.

HORNER

Do not take it ill, I cannot make china for you all, but I will
have a roll-wagon for you too, another time.

SQUEAMISH

Thank you, dear toad.   205

LADY FIDGET (*To* HORNER, *aside*)

What do you mean by that promise?

HORNER (*Apart to* LADY FIDGET)

Alas, she has an innocent, literal understanding.

OLD LADY SQUEAMISH

Poor Master Horner, he has enough to do to please you all,
I see.

HORNER

Ay, madam, you see how they use me.   210

OLD LADY SQUEAMISH

Poor gentleman, I pity you.

HORNER

I thank you madam. I could never find pity but from such
reverend ladies as you are. The young ones will never spare
a man.

SQUEAMISH

Come, come, beast, and go dine with us, for we shall want   215
a man at ombre after dinner.

HORNER

That's all their use of me, madam, you see.

SQUEAMISH

Come, sloven, I'll lead you, to be sure of you.

> *Pulls him by the cravat*

OLD LADY SQUEAMISH

Alas, poor man, how she tugs him! Kiss, kiss her!
That's the way to make such nice women quiet.   220

---

204   *roll-wagon* a cylindrical china vase, somewhat phallic in appearance. See R. J. Charleston,
        Apollo, vol. 65 (1957), 251.
205–7 As Horner replies to Lady Fidget in an aside, her question is presumably an aside to him.
        But in Q1 the sd '*To* Horn, *aside*' is moved to the line above, presumably to save space,
        and this arrangement persists in Q2–5, O, even where there is no need to save space.
        Hence some editors give the aside to Mrs Squeamish, but there seems to be no reason
        why she should not speak openly.
215–6 *want a man at ombre* See II.i. 473 and note.
220   *nice* fastidious about reputation

HORNER

No, madam, that remedy is worse than the torment. They know I dare suffer anything rather than do it.

OLD LADY SQUEAMISH

Prithee kiss her, and I'll give you her picture in little, that you admired so last night. Prithee, do!

HORNER

Well, nothing but that could bribe me. I love a woman only   225
in effigy, and good painting, as much as I hate them. I'll do't,
for I could adore the devil well painted.

Kisses Mrs SQUEAMISH

SQUEAMISH

Foh! you filthy toad! Nay, now I've done jesting.

OLD LADY SQUEAMISH

Ha, ha, ha! I told you so.

SQUEAMISH

Foh! a kiss of his –   230

SIR JASPAR

Has no more hurt in't than one of my spaniel's.

SQUEAMISH

Nor no more good neither.

QUACK (*Behind*)

I will now believe anything he tells me.

Enter PINCHWIFE

LADY FIDGET

O Lord, here's a man! Sir Jaspar, my mask, my mask! I would not be seen here for the world.   235

SIR JASPAR

What, not when I am with you?

LADY FIDGET

No, no, my honour – let's be gone.

SQUEAMISH

Oh, grandmother, let us be gone. Make haste, make haste! I know not how he may censure us!

LADY FIDGET

Be found in the lodging of anything like a man! Away!   240

Exeunt SIR JASPAR, LADY FIDGET,
OLD LADY SQUEAMISH, *Mrs* SQUEAMISH

223 *picture in little* miniature

QUACK (*Behind*)

What's here, another cuckold? He looks like one, and none
else sure have any business with him.

HORNER

Well, what brings my dear friend hither?

PINCHWIFE

Your impertinency.

HORNER

My impertinency! Why, you gentlemen that have got   245
handsome wives think you have a privilege of saying
anything to your friends, and are as brutish as if you were our
creditors.

PINCHWIFE

No, sir, I'll ne'er trust you any way.

HORNER

But why not, dear Jack? Why diffide in me thou know'st so   250
well?

PINCHWIFE

Because I do know you so well.

HORNER

Ha'n't I been always thy friend, honest Jack, always ready to
serve thee, in love or battle, before thou wert married, and am
so still?   255

PINCHWIFE

I believe so. You would be my second now indeed.

HORNER

Well, then, dear Jack, why so unkind, so grum, so
strange to me? Come, prithee kiss me, dear rogue. Gad,
I was always, I say, and am still as much thy servant
as –   260

PINCHWIFE

As I am yours, sir. What, you would send a kiss to my wife, is
that it?

---

250 *diffide in* distrust
254 *battle* duels; or so understood by Pinchwife, l. 256
258 *strange* distant
      kiss me On this custom among fashionable gentlemen the Orange-Woman in *The Man
      of Mode* comments: 'Lord what a filthy trick these men have got of kissing one another!
      She spits' (I.i. 61–2).

HORNER

So, there 'tis. A man can't show his friendship to a
married man, but presently he talks of his wife to you.
Prithee, let thy wife alone, and let thee and I be all one,   265
as we were wont. What, thou art as shy of my kindness
as a Lombard Street alderman of a courtier's civility at
Locket's.

PINCHWIFE

But you are overkind to me, as kind as if I were your
cuckold already. Yet I must confess you ought to be kind and   270
civil to me, since I am so kind, so civil to you, as to bring
    this. Look you there, sir.   *Delivers him a letter*

HORNER

What is't?

PINCHWIFE

Only a love letter, sir.

HORNER

From whom? – How! this is from your wife!   (*Reads*)   275
Hum – and hum –

PINCHWIFE

Even from my wife, sir. Am I not wondrous kind and civil to
you now too? (*Aside*) But you'll not think her so!

HORNER (*Aside*)

Ha! Is this a trick of his or hers?

PINCHWIFE

The gentleman's surprised, I find. What, you expected a kinder   280
letter?

HORNER

No, faith, not I, how could I?

PINCHWIFE

Yes, yes, I'm sure you did. A man so well made as you are
must needs be disappointed, if the women declare not their
passion at first sight or opportunity.   285

---

265 *all* one friends
266 *shy* suspicious
267 *Lombard Street alderman* a banker or moneylender, who would suspect a courtier of
     avoiding a debt, or wanting a loan, or trying to cuckold him
268 *Locket's* fashionable restaurant
269–70   See I.i. 434.

HORNER (*Aside*)

But what should this mean? Stay, the postscript.(*Reads*)
'Be sure you love me whatsoever my husband says to the
contrary, and let him not see this, lest he should come home
and pinch me, or kill my squirrel'. It seems he knows not what the
letter contains.   290

PINCHWIFE

Come, ne'er wonder at it so much.

HORNER

Faith, I can't help it.

PINCHWIFE

Now, I think I have deserved your infinite friendship and
kindness and have showed myself sufficiently an obliging friend
and husband. Am I not so, to bring a letter from my wife to   295
her gallant?

HORNER

Ay, the devil take me, art thou the most obliging, kind friend
and husband in the world, ha, ha!

PINCHWIFE

Well, you may be merry, sir, but in short I must tell you,sir,
my honour will suffer no jesting.   300

HORNER

What dost thou mean?

PINCHWIFE

Does the letter want a comment? Then know, sir, though
I have been so civil a husband as to bring you a letter from my
wife, to let you kiss and court her to my face, I will not be a
cuckold, sir, I will not.   305

HORNER

Thou art mad with jealousy. I never saw thy wife in my life,
but at the play yesterday, and I know not if it were she or no. I
court her, kiss her!

PINCHWIFE

I will not be a cuckold, I say. There will be danger in making
me a cuckold.   310

HORNER

Why, wert thou not well cured of thy last clap?

289 *squirrel* a fashionable pet
299 *merry* facetious
311 *clap* gonorrhoea

PINCHWIFE

I wear a sword.

HORNER

It should be taken from thee lest thou should'st do thyself
a mischief with it. Thou art mad, man.

PINCHWIFE

As mad as I am, and as merry as you are, I must have more   315
reason from you ere we part. I say again, though you kissed
and courted last night my wife in man's clothes, as she confesses
in her letter –

HORNER (*Aside*)

Ha!

PINCHWIFE

Both she and I say, you must not design it again, for you have   320
mistaken your woman, as you have done your man.

HORNER (*Aside*)

Oh! I understand something now. – Was that thy wife?
Why would'st thou not tell me 'twas she? Faith, my freedom
with her was your fault, not mine.

PINCHWIFE (*Aside*)

Faith, so 'twas.   325

HORNER

Fie! I'd never do't to a woman before her husband's face,
sure.

PINCHWIFE

But I had rather you should do't to my wife before my face
than behind my back, and that you shall never do.

HORNER

No – you will hinder me.   330

PINCHWIFE

If I would not hinder you, you see by her letter, she
would.

HORNER

Well, I must e'en acquiesce then, and be contented with what
she writes.

316   *reason* explanation
322   *something* i.e., that Pinchwife thinks he has brought a different letter. He pretends he has
      just understood that it was Mrs Pinchwife in man's clothes.
330   sarcastic reference to Pinchwife's boasted sword (l. 312).

PINCHWIFE

I'll assure you 'twas voluntarily writ. I had no hand in't, you   335
may believe me.

HORNER

I do believe thee, faith.

PINCHWIFE

And believe her too, for she's an innocent creature, has no
dissembling in her; and so fare you well, sir.

HORNER

Pray, however, present my humble service to her, and tell   340
her I will obey her letter to a tittle, and fulfil her desires,
be what they will, or with what difficulty soever I do't,
and you shall be no more jealous of me, I warrant her, and
you –

PINCHWIFE

Well, then, fare you well, and play with any man's   345
honour but mine, kiss any man's wife but mine, and
welcome.   *Exit* PINCHWIFE

HORNER

Ha, ha, ha! Doctor.

QUACK

It seems he has not heard the report of you, or does not
believe it.   350

HORNER

Ha, ha! Now, doctor, what think you?

QUACK

Pray let's see the letter – hum – (*Reads the letter*) 'for – dear –
love you' –

HORNER

I wonder how she could contrive it! What say'st thou to't?
'Tis an original.   355

QUACK

So are your cuckolds, too, originals, for they are like no other
common cuckolds, and I will henceforth believe it not

341 *to a tittle* in every particular
355 *an original* her own work, not a copy. The same word is used by Ergaste of Isabelle's letter in *L'École des Maris* II.v.

impossible for you to cuckold the Grand Signior amidst his
guards of eunuchs, that I say –

HORNER

And I say for the letter, 'tis the first love letter that ever was   360
without flames, darts, fates, destinies, lying and dissembling
in't.

Enter SPARKISH *pulling in* PINCHWIFE

SPARKISH

Come back, you are a pretty brother-in-law, neither go to
church, nor to dinner with your sister bride.

PINCHWIFE

My sister denies her marriage, and you see is gone away from   365
you dissatisfied.

SPARKISH

Pshaw! upon a foolish scruple that our parson was not
in lawful orders, and did not say all the Common
Prayer. But 'tis her modesty only, I believe. But let
women be never so modest the first day, they'll be sure to   370
come to themselves by night, and I shall have enough of
her then. In the meantime, Harry Horner, you must
dine with me. I keep my wedding at my aunt's in the
Piazza.

HORNER

Thy wedding! What stale maid has lived to despair of a   375
husband, or what young one of a gallant?

SPARKISH

Oh, your servant, sir – this gentleman's sister then – no stale
maid.

HORNER

I'm sorry for't.

PINCHWIFE (*Aside*)

How comes he so concerned for her?   380

SPARKISH

You sorry for't? Why, do you know any ill by her?

358   *Grand Signior* Sultan of Turkey; also mentioned at II.i. 471–2
359   *that I say* that's what I say (Dixon)
368–9 *Common Prayer* marriage service in the Anglican *Book of Common Prayer*
374   *Piazza* arcade near Covent Garden. V.iii. is located there.
375   *stale* past her best
      Thy wedding! Horner knows about the wedding but had thought (ll. 382–4 below)
      Harcourt might have prevented it.

HORNER

No, I know none but by thee. 'Tis for her sake, not
yours, and another man's sake that might have hoped, I
thought –

SPARKISH

Another man! Another man! What is his name?   385

HORNER

Nay, since 'tis past he shall be nameless. (*Aside*) Poor Harcourt!
I am sorry thou hast missed her.

PINCHWIFE (*Aside*)

He seems to be much troubled at the match.

SPARKISH

Prithee tell me – nay, you shan't go, brother.

PINCHWIFE

I must of necessity, but I'll come to you to dinner.   390

Exit PINCHWIFE

SPARKISH

But Harry, what, have I rival in my wife already? But
with all my heart, for he may be of use to me hereafter.
For though my hunger is now my sauce, and I can fall on
heartily without, but the time will come when a rival will
be as good sauce for a married man to a wife as an orange   395
to veal.

HORNER

O thou damned rogue, thou hast set my teeth on edge with
thy orange!

SPARKISH

Then let's to dinner – there I was with you again.
Come.   400

HORNER

But who dines with thee?

SPARKISH

My friends and relations, my brother Pinchwife, you see,
of your acquaintance.

HORNER

And his wife?

SPARKISH

No, gad, he'll ne'er let her come amongst us good   405

387 *missed* lost
399 *was with you* had you

[153]

fellows. Your stingy country coxcomb keeps his wife from his friends as he does his little firkin of ale for his own drinking, and a gentleman can't get a smack on't. But his servants, when his back is turned, broach it at their pleasures, and dust it away, ha, ha, ha! Gad, I am witty, 410 I think, considering I was married today, by the world. But come –

HORNER

No, I will not dine with you, unless you can fetch her too.

SPARKISH

Pshaw! what pleasure canst thou have with women now 415 Harry?

HORNER

My eyes are not gone; I love a good prospect yet, and will not dine with you unless she does too. Go fetch her, therefore, but do not tell her husband 'tis for my sake.

SPARKISH

Well, I'll go try what I can do. In the meantime come away to 420 my aunt's lodging, 'tis in the way to Pinchwife's.

HORNER [*Aside to* QUACK]

The poor woman has called for aid, and stretched forth her hand, doctor. I cannot but help her over the pale out of the briars.   *Exeunt* SPARKISH, HORNER, QUACK

Act IV, Scene iv

The scene changes to PINCHWIFE'*s house*
Mrs PINCHWIFE *alone leaning on her elbow. A table,*
pen, ink, and paper

MRS PINCHWIFE

Well, 'tis e'en so, I have got the London disease they call

---

407 *firkin* cask
408 *smack* taste
410 *dust it away* toss it off; with a sexual innuendo
423 *pale* (literally) fence, (metaphorically) boundary, especially boundary of civilisation
424 *briars* (literally) prickly bushes, (metaphorically) difficulties, 'with conscious reference to the literal sense' (*OED* brier *sb.*[1] 4)

love. I am sick of my husband, and for my gallant. I have
heard this distemper called a fever, but methinks 'tis liker
an ague, for when I think of my husband I tremble
and am in a cold sweat, and have inclinations to vomit,   5
but when I think of my gallant, dear Master Horner,
my hot fit comes and I am all in a fever, indeed, and
as in other fevers my own chamber is tedious to me,
and I would fain be removed to his, and then methinks
I should be well. Ah, poor Master Horner! Well, I cannot,   10
will not stay here. Therefore I'll make an end of my
letter to him, which shall be a finer letter than
my last, because I have studied it like anything. Oh, sick,
sick!   *Takes the pen and writes*

> *Enter* PINCHWIFE, *who seeing her writing*
> *steals softly behind her, and looking over her shoulder,*
> *snatches the paper from her*

PINCHWIFE
What, writing more letters?   15
MRS PINCHWIFE
O Lord, bud, why d'ye fright me so?
                      She offers to run out; he stops her and reads
PINCHWIFE
How's this! Nay, you shall not stir, madam. 'Dear, dear,
dear Master Horner' – very well! – I have taught you to
write letters to good purpose – but let's see't – 'First, I
am to beg your pardon for my boldness in writing to   20
you, which I'd have you to know I would not have done,
had not you said first you loved me so extremely, which
if you do, you will never suffer me to lie in the arms of
another man, whom I loathe, nauseate, and detest' – Now you
can write these filthy words! But what follows? – 'Therefore   25
I hope you will speedily find some way to
free me from this unfortunate match, which was never, I

2 *for* i.e., sick for
3 *distemper* unbalanced state, disease
4 *ague* type of fever recognised by successive cold shivering and hot feverish symptoms
13 *studied* thought about
    like anything very hard; vulgarism
27 *match* This usually means an engagement rather than a marriage; seems a bit
    disingenuous.

assure you, of my choice, but I'm afraid 'tis already too
far gone. However, if you love me, as I do you, you will
try what you can do, but you must help me away before   30
tomorrow, or else, alas, I shall be for ever out of your
reach, for I can defer no longer our' – (*The letter
concludes*) 'Our'? What is to follow 'our'? Speak, what?
Our journey into the country I suppose? Oh, woman,
damned woman! And love, damned love, their old   35
tempter! For this is one of his miracles. In a moment
he can make those blind that could see, and those see
that were blind, those dumb that could speak, and those
prattle who were dumb before; nay, what is more than
all, make these dough-baked, senseless, indocile animals,   40
women, too hard for us, their politic lords and rulers,
in a moment. But make an end of your letter and
then I'll make an end of you thus, and all my plagues
together.   *Draws his sword*

MRS PINCHWIFE

O Lord, O Lord, you are such a passionate man, bud.   45

Enter SPARKISH

SPARKISH

How now, what's here to do?

PINCHWIFE

This fool here now!

SPARKISH

What, drawn upon your wife? You should never do that,
but at night in the dark, when you can't hurt her! This
is my sister-in-law, is it not? (*Pulls aside her handkerchief*)   50
Ay, faith, e'en our country Margery; one may know her.
Come, she and you must go dine with me; dinner's
ready, come. But where's my wife? Is she not come home yet?
Where is she?

PINCHWIFE

Making you a cuckold; 'tis that they all do, as soon as   55
they can.

36–9 paraphrase of Isaiah 35:5–6
  40 *dough-baked* half-baked
     indocile hard to teach
  41 *politic* lawful
  48 *drawn* both having a sword drawn and ready for sex; play on words
  50 sd *handkerchief* head-dress

SPARKISH

What, the wedding day? No, a wife that designs to make a cully of her husband will be sure to let him win the first stake of love, by the world. But come, they stay dinner for us. Come, I'll lead down our Margery.   60

PINCHWIFE

No! – Sir, go, we'll follow you.

SPARKISH

I will not wag without you.

PINCHWIFE [*Aside*]

This coxcomb is a sensible torment to me amidst the greatest in the world.

SPARKISH

Come, come, Madam Margery.   65

PINCHWIFE

No, I'll lead her my way. (*Leads her to t'other door and locks her in and returns*) What, would you treat your friends with mine, for want of your own wife? (*Aside*) I am contented my rage should take breath.

SPARKISH [*Aside*]

I told Horner this.   70

PINCHWIFE

Come now.

SPARKISH

Lord, how shy you are of your wife! But let me tell you, brother, we men of wit have amongst us a saying that cuckolding, like the smallpox, comes with a fear, and you may keep your wife as much as you will out of danger   75 of infection, but if her constitution incline her to't, she'll have it sooner or later, by the world, say they.

PINCHWIFE (*Aside*)

What a thing is a cuckold, that every fool can make him ridiculous! – Well sir, but let me advise you, now you

58   *cully* Q1–4, O (cuckold Q5) dupe, especially cuckold
61   SP PINCHWIFE ed. (*Mrs. Pin.* Q1–5, O)
62   *wag* go
63   *sensible* painful
65   *Madam Margery* form of address implying high social status; Sparkish at his most ceremonious
72   *how shy you are of* how cautious you are about
74   *comes with a fear* is brought on by fearing it

are come to be concerned, because you suspect the   80
danger, not to neglect the means to prevent it, especially
when the greatest share of the malady will light upon your own
head, for –
  Hows'e'er the kind wife's belly comes to swell,
  The husband breeds for her, and first is ill.   85
                                              [*Exeunt*]

Act V, Scene i

PINCHWIFE'*s house*
Enter PINCHWIFE *and* MRS PINCHWIFE
A table and candle

PINCHWIFE

Come, take the pen and make an end of the letter, just
as you intended. If you are false in a tittle, I shall soon
perceive it, and punish you with this as you deserve. (*Lays
his hand on his sword*) Write what was to follow -let's
see – 'You must make haste and help me away before   5
tomorrow, or else I shall be for ever out of your
reach, for I can defer no longer our' – What follows
'our'?

MRS PINCHWIFE

Must all out then, bud? (MRS PINCHWIFE *takes the pen and
writes*) Look you there, then.   10

PINCHWIFE

Let's see – 'For I can defer no longer our wedding. Your
slighted Alithea'. – What's the meaning of this? My sister's
name to't? Speak, unriddle!

MRS PINCHWIFE

Yes, indeed, bud.

PINCHWIFE

But why her name to't? Speak – speak I say!   15

MRS PINCHWIFE

Ay, but you'll tell her then again. If you would not tell her
again –

---

85   *breeds for her* grows cuckold's horns on her behalf

16   *tell her then again* repeat it to her

PINCHWIFE

I will not; I am stunned; my head turns round. Speak!

MRS PINCHWIFE

Won't you tell her indeed, and indeed?

PINCHWIFE

No, speak I say.   20

MRS PINCHWIFE

She'll be angry with me, but I had rather she should be angry
with me than you, bud. And to tell you the truth 'twas
she made me write the letter, and taught me what I should
write.

PINCHWIFE

Ha! (*Aside*) I thought the style was somewhat better than   25
her own. – But how could she come to you to teach you,
since I had locked you up alone?

MRS PINCHWIFE

Oh, through the keyhole, bud.

PINCHWIFE

But why should she make you write a letter for her to him,
since she can write herself?   30

MRS PINCHWIFE

Why, she said because – for I was unwilling to do it.

PINCHWIFE

Because what – because?

MRS PINCHWIFE

Because, lest Master Horner should be cruel and refuse her,
or vain afterwards, and show the letter, she might disown it,
the hand not being hers.   35

PINCHWIFE (*Aside*)

How's this? Ha – then I think I shall come to myself again.
This changeling could not invent this lie, but if she could,
why should she? She might think I should soon discover
it – stay – now I think on't too, Horner said he was sorry
she had married Sparkish, and her disowning her marriage   40
to me makes me think she has evaded it for Horner's sake.
Yet why should she take this course? But men in love
are fools; women may well be so. – But hark you, madam,

25 sd (*Aside*) Q4–5, O (Q1–3 *omit*)
26 *but how* Q1–3 (Q4–5, O *omit*)
38 *might* would surely

your sister went out in the morning and I have not seen her
within since.   45

MRS PINCHWIFE

Alackaday, she has been crying all day above, it seems, in a
corner.

PINCHWIFE

Where is she? Let me speak with her.

MRS PINCHWIFE (*Aside*)

O Lord, then he'll discover all! – Pray hold, bud. What, d'ye mean
to discover me? She'll know I have told you then. Pray bud,   50
let me talk with her first.

PINCHWIFE

I must speak with her to know whether Horner ever made
her any promise; and whether she be married to Sparkish
or no.

MRS PINCHWIFE

Pray, dear bud, don't, till I have spoken with her and told her   55
that I have told you all, for she'll kill me else.

PINCHWIFE

Go then, and bid her come out to me.

MRS PINCHWIFE

Yes, yes, bud.

PINCHWIFE

Let me see –

MRS PINCHWIFE [*Aside*]

I'll go, but she is not within to come to him. I have just   60
got time to know of Lucy her maid, who first set me on
work, what lie I shall tell next, for I am e'en at my wit's
end!   *Exit* MRS PINCHWIFE

PINCHWIFE

Well, I resolve it; Horner shall have her. I'd rather give him
my sister than lend him my wife, and such an alliance will   65
prevent his pretensions to my wife, sure. I'll make him of
kin to her, and then he won't care for her.

50 *discover* betray

MRS PINCHWIFE *returns*

MRS PINCHWIFE

O Lord, bud, I told you what anger you would make me
with my sister.

PINCHWIFE

Won't she come hither?   70

MRS PINCHWIFE

No, no, alackaday, she's ashamed to look you in the face,
and she says if you go in to her, she'll run away downstairs,
and shamefully go herself to Master Horner, who has promised
her marriage, she says, and she will have no other, so
she won't.   75

PINCHWIFE

Did he so – promise her marriage? Then she shall have
no other. Go tell her so, and if she will come and discourse
with me a little concerning the means, I will about it
immediately. Go!   (*Exit* MRS PINCHWIFE)
His estate is equal to Sparkish's, and his extraction as   80
much better than his as his parts are. But my chief reason
is, I'd rather be of kin to him by the name of brother-in-law
than that of cuckold.

Enter MRS PINCHWIFE

Well, what says she now?

MRS PINCHWIFE

Why, she says she would only have you lead her to Horner's 85
lodging – with whom she first will discourse the matter before
she talk with you, which yet she cannot do. For alack,
poor creature, she says she can't so much as look you in
the face, therefore she'll come to you in a mask. And you
must excuse her if she make you no answer to any question   90
of yours till you have brought her to Master Horner. And
if you will not chide her nor question her she'll come out
to you immediately.

---

81   *parts* abilities. A deliberate pun on private parts is possible, as Pinchwife does not suppose Horner a eunuch, but it is not probable, as the word has no suggestive context and
is not repeated. Compare II.i. 276–7.

87   *talk* Q1–3 (talks Q4–5, O). Perhaps Mrs Pinchwife's grammar should be preserved; *yet*
as yet

PINCHWIFE

Let her come. I will not speak a word to her, nor require
a word from her.   95

MRS PINCHWIFE

Oh, I forgot – besides, she says, she cannot look you in the
face, though through a mask, therefore would desire you to
put out the candle.

PINCHWIFE

I agree to all; let her make haste.   (*Exit* MRS PINCHWIFE)
There 'tis out. (*Puts out the candle*) My case is something   100
better; I'd rather fight with Horner for not lying with
my sister than for lying with my wife, and of the two I
had rather find my sister too forward than my wife. I
expected no other from her free education, as she calls
it, and her passion for the town. Well, wife and sister   105
are names which make us expect love and duty, pleasure
and comfort, but we find 'em plagues and torments,
and are equally, though differently troublesome to their
keeper; for we have as much ado to get people to lie
with our sisters as to keep 'em from lying with our   110
wives.

Enter MRS PINCHWIFE *masked, and in hoods and scarves,*
and a night gown and petticoat of ALITHEA'*s,*
in the dark

What, are you come, sister? Let us go then – but first let
me lock up my wife. Mistress Margery, where are you?

MRS PINCHWIFE

Here, bud.

PINCHWIFE

Come hither, that I may lock you up. (MRS PINCHWIFE   115
gives him her hand, but when he lets her go, she steals softly on

---

100 sd *puts out the candle* This makes the stage symbolically dark, so that he cannot see his
wife is disguised as Alithea, but the audience can.
101 *not lying with* refusing to marry. Pinchwife uses the same gross idiom at I.i. 321.
111 sd *scarves* ornamental strips of silk
night gown loose gown or wrap, not necessarily worn only indoors
petticoat skirt

t'other side of him) Get you in. (*Locks the door*) Come, sister,
where are you now?

[MRS PINCHWIFE] *is led away by him for his sister Alithea*

Act V, Scene ii

The scene changes to HORNER's *lodging*
QUACK, HORNER

QUACK
What, all alone? Not so much as one of your cuckolds here,
nor one of their wives! They use to take their turns with you, as
if they were to watch you.

HORNER
Yes, it often happens that a cuckold is but his wife's spy,
and is more upon family duty when he is with her gallant   5
abroad, hindering his pleasure, than when he is at home
with her, playing the gallant. But the hardest duty a married
woman imposes upon a lover is keeping her husband
company always.

QUACK
And his fondness wearies you almost as soon as hers.   10

HORNER
A pox! keeping a cuckold company after you have had his
wife is as tiresome as the company of a country squire to
a witty fellow of the town, when he has got all his
money.

QUACK
And as at first a man makes a friend of the husband to get the   15
wife, so at last you are fain to fall out with the wife to be rid of the
husband.

HORNER
Ay, most cuckold-makers are true courtiers. When once a poor
man has cracked his credit for 'em, they can't abide to come
near him.   20

118 sd *for* in mistake for

2 *use to* are accustomed to
5 *more upon family duty* doing more for family honour
19 *cracked his credit* (literally) bankrupted himself; (metaphorically)
    become a cuckold

[163]

QUACK

But at first, to draw him in, are so sweet, so kind, so dear, just as you are to Pinchwife. But what becomes of that intrigue with his wife?

HORNER

A pox! He's as surly as an alderman that has been bit, and since he's so coy, his wife's kindness is in vain, for she's a silly innocent.   25

QUACK

Did she not send you a letter by him?

HORNER

Yes, but that's a riddle I have not yet solved. Allow the poor creature to be willing, she is silly too, and he keeps her up so close –   30

QUACK

Yes, so close that he makes her but the more willing, and adds but revenge to her love, which two, when met, seldom fail of satisfying each other one way or other.

HORNER

What! here's the man we are talking of, I think.

Enter PINCHWIFE *leading in his wife, masked, muffled, and in her sister's gown*

Pshaw!   35

QUACK

Bringing his wife to you is the next thing to bringing a love letter from her.

HORNER

What means this?

PINCHWIFE

The last time, you know, sir, I brought you a love letter. Now you see a mistress. I think you'll say I am a civil man   40 to you.

HORNER

Ay, the devil take me, will I say thou art the civillest man I ever met with, and I have known some. I fancy I understand

24 *bit* tricked
25 *coy* cautious
    kindness readiness for sex. See also III.ii. 540.

[164]

thee now better than I did the letter. But hark thee, in thy
ear –   45

PINCHWIFE
What?

HORNER
Nothing but the usual question, man; is she sound, on thy
word?

PINCHWIFE
What, you take her for a wench, and me for a pimp?

HORNER
Pshaw! wench and pimp, paw words. I know thou art an   50
honest fellow, and hast a great acquaintance amongst the
ladies, and perhaps hast made love for me rather than let me make
love to thy wife –

PINCHWIFE
Come sir; in short, I am for no fooling.

HORNER
Nor I neither; therefore prithee let's see her face   55
presently. Make her show, man! Art thou sure I don't know
her?

PINCHWIFE
I am sure you do know her.

HORNER
A pox! why dost thou bring her to me then?

PINCHWIFE
Because she's a relation of mine –   60

HORNER
Is she, faith, man? Then thou art still more civil and obliging,
dear rogue.

PINCHWIFE
– who desired me to bring her to you.

HORNER
Then she is obliging, dear rogue.

PINCHWIFE
You'll make her welcome, for my sake, I hope.   65

HORNER
I hope she is handsome enough to make herself welcome.
Prithee, let her unmask.

47 *sound* free from pox
50 *paw* improper, naughty, or obscene (*OED*)
56 *show* show herself

PINCHWIFE

Do you speak to her. She would never be ruled by me.

HORNER

Madam – (MRS PINCHWIFE *whispers to* HORNER) She says she must
speak with me in private. Withdraw, prithee.   70

PINCHWIFE (*Aside*)

She's unwilling, it seems, I should know all her undecent
conduct in this business. – Well, then, I'll leave you together,
and hope when I am gone you'll agree. If not, you and I
shan't agree, sir.

HORNER [*Aside*]

What means the fool? – If she and I agree, 'tis no matter what   75
you and I do.   *Whispers to* MRS PINCHWIFE *who makes signs
with her hand for him to be gone*

PINCHWIFE [*Aside*]

In the meantime I'll fetch a parson, and find out
Sparkish and disabuse him. – You would have me fetch
a parson, would you not? Well, then – [*Aside*] Now I
think I am rid of her, and shall have no more trouble   80
with her. Our sisters and daughters, like usurers' money,
are safest when put out, but our wives, like their
writings, never safe but in our closets under lock and
key.   *Exit* PINCHWIFE

Enter BOY

BOY

Sir Jaspar Fidget, sir, is coming up.   [*Exit* BOY]   85

69–91 Q1–5, O substantially agree in their stage directions, but the stage business is not obvious. I think Mrs Pinchwife and Horner detach themselves from Pinchwife and whisper
together; Pinchwife addresses himself partly to the audience and partly to them. Horner
after his aside at l. 75 speaks to Pinchwife and then whispers to Mrs Pinchwife, who makes
signs for 'him' (i.e., Pinchwife) to be gone throughout Pinchwife's exit speech. After the
boy has announced Sir Jaspar Fidget, Horner addresses first Quack and then Mrs Pinchwife, who is hustled into the bedroom.

76 sd *hand* Q1–4, O (*hands* Q5)

82 *put out* invested

82–3 *their writings* the usurers' documents

[166]

HORNER [*Aside to* QUACK]

Here's the trouble of a cuckold, now, we are talking of. A pox on him! Has he not enough to do to hinder his wife's sport, but he must other women's too? – Step in here madam.   *Exit* MRS PINCHWIFE

Enter SIR JASPAR

SIR JASPAR

My best and dearest friend.   90

HORNER [*Aside to* QUACK]

The old style, doctor. – Well, be short, for I am busy. What would your impertinent wife have now?

SIR JASPAR

Well guessed, i'faith, for I do come from her.

HORNER

To invite me to supper? Tell her I can't come. Go.

SIR JASPAR

Nay, now you are out, faith, for my lady and the whole knot   95
of the virtuous gang, as they call themselves, are resolved
upon a frolic of coming to you tonight in a masquerade,
and are all dressed already.

HORNER

I shan't be at home.

SIR JASPAR (*Aside*)

Lord, how churlish he is to women! – Nay, prithee   100
don't disappoint 'em, they'll think 'tis my fault, prithee
don't. I'll send in the banquet and the fiddles. But make
no noise on't, for the poor virtuous rogues would not
have it known for the world, that they go a-
masquerading, and they would come to no man's ball but   105
yours.

86 *are* were; historic present. They were talking of Sir Jaspar in ll. 1–22.
91 *the old style* the sort of address we would expect
96 *knot* group of conspirators; *gang* society, not as pejorative a term as it is now
97 *a masquerade* Q1–3 (masquerade Q4–5, O)
102 *banquet* refreshments
     fiddles fiddlers, as at II.i. 82. Possibly Sir Jaspar's musicians play for the dance of cuck-
     olds at the end of V.iv.
105 *ball* party, as at II.i. 82

HORNER

Well, well – get you gone, and tell 'em, if they come, 'twill be
at the peril of their honour and yours.

SIR JASPAR

He, he, he! We'll trust you for that, farewell.   *Exit* SIR JASPAR

HORNER

Doctor, anon, you too shall be my guest,   110
But now I'm going to a private feast.   [*Exeunt*]

Act V, Scene iii

The scene changes to the Piazza of Covent Garden
SPARKISH, PINCHWIFE

SPARKISH (*With the letter in his hand*)

But who would have thought a woman could have been
false to me? By the world, I could not have thought it.

PINCHWIFE

You were for giving and taking liberty; she has taken it
only, sir, now you find in that letter. You are a frank
person, and so is she, you see there.   5

SPARKISH

Nay, if this be her hand – for I never saw it.

PINCHWIFE

'Tis no matter whether that be her hand or no. I am
sure this hand, at her desire, led her to Master Horner,
with whom I left her just now, to go fetch a parson to
'em, at their desire too, to deprive you of her for ever,   10
for it seems yours was but a mock marriage.

SPARKISH

Indeed, she would needs have it that 'twas Harcourt
himself in a parson's habit that married us, but I'm sure
he told me 'twas his brother Ned.

---

1 sd *the letter*, i.e., that written by Mrs Pinchwife but signed Pinchwife has now told Sparkish it was written by Alithea.
4 *frank* generous. See III.ii. 360.
6 *hand* handwriting

PINCHWIFE

Oh, there 'tis out, and you were deceived, not she, for   15
you are such a frank person – but I must be gone. You'll
find her at Master Horner's. Go and believe your eyes.

Exit PINCHWIFE

SPARKISH

Nay, I'll to her, and call her as many crocodiles, sirens,
harpies, and other heathenish names as a poet would do
a mistress who had refused to hear his suit, nay more,   20
his verses on her. But stay, is not that she following a
torch at t'other end of the Piazza? And from Horner's
certainly – 'tis so.

Enter ALITHEA *following a torch, and* LUCY *behind*

You are well met, madam, though you don't think so.
What, you have made a short visit to Master Horner,   25
but I suppose you'll return to him presently. By that
time the parson can be with him.

ALITHEA

Master Horner, and the parson, sir?

SPARKISH

Come, madam, no more dissembling, no more jilting,
for I am no more a frank person.   30

ALITHEA

How's this?

LUCY (*Aside*)

So, 'twill work, I see

SPARKISH

Could you find out no easy country fool to abuse?
None but me, a gentleman of wit and pleasure about the
town? But it was your pride to be too hard for a man of   35
parts, unworthy false woman! False as a friend that
lends a man money to lose. False as dice, who undo
those that trust all they have to 'em.

LUCY (*Aside*)

He has been a great bubble by his similes, as they say.

---

18 *crocodiles* hypocrites
22 *torch* linkboy with torch
29 *jilting* deceiving
39 Judging by his similes, he has been tricked many times, as they say.

ALITHEA

You have been too merry, sir, at your wedding dinner,   40
sure.

SPARKISH

What, d'ye mock me too?

ALITHEA

Or you have been deluded.

SPARKISH

By you!

ALITHEA

Let me understand you.   45

SPARKISH

Have you the confidence – I should call it something
else, since you know your guilt – to stand my just
reproaches? You did not write an impudent letter to
Master Horner, who I find now has clubbed with you in
deluding me with his aversion for women, that I might   50
not, forsooth, suspect him for my rival?

LUCY (*Aside*)

D'ye think the gentleman can be jealous now, madam?

ALITHEA

I write a letter to Master Horner!

SPARKISH

Nay, madam, do not deny it. Your brother showed it
me just now, and told me likewise he left you at   55
Horner's lodging to fetch a parson to marry you to him.
And I wish you joy, madam, joy, joy! and to him, too,
much joy! and to myself more joy for not marrying you!

ALITHEA (*Aside*)

So I find my brother would break off the match, and I
can consent to't, since I see this gentleman can be made   60
jealous. – O Lucy, by his rude usage and jealousy, he
makes me almost afraid I am married to him. Art thou
sure 'twas Harcourt himself and no parson that married
us?

SPARKISH

No, madam, I thank you. I suppose that was a contrivance   65
too of Master Horner's and yours, to make Harcourt play
the parson. But I would, as little as you, have him one now,
no, not for the world, for shall I tell you another truth?
I never had any passion for you till now, for now I hate

you. 'Tis true I might have married your portion, as   70
other men of parts of the town do sometimes; and
so your servant. And to show my unconcernedness,
I'll come to your wedding and resign you with as much
joy as I would a stale wench to a newcully. Nay, with
as much joy as I would after the first night, if I had   75
been married to you. There's for you, and so your servant,
servant.   *Exit* SPARKISH

ALITHEA

How was I deceived in a man!

LUCY

You'll believe, then, a fool may be made jealous now?
For that easiness in him that suffers him to be led by a   80
wife, will likewise permit him to be persuaded against
her by others.

ALITHEA

But marry Master Horner! My brother does not intend
it, sure. If I thought he did, I would take thy advice and
Master Harcourt for my husband. And now I wish that   85
if there be any over-wise woman of the town, who, like
me, would marry a fool for fortune, liberty, or title: first,
that her husband may love play, and be a cully to all the
town, but her, and suffer none but fortune to be mistress
of his purse. Then, if for liberty, that he may send her   90
into the country under the conduct of some housewifely
mother-in-law. And, if for title, may the world give 'em
none but that of cuckold.

LUCY

And for her greater curse, madam, may he not deserve
it.   95

ALITHEA

Away, impertinent! – Is not this my Old Lady
Lanterlu's?

72 *and so your servant* He takes leave, but has afterthoughts.
76 *and so your servant, servant* He takes leave again, but adds a mocking quibble on 'servant' in the sense of lover.
97 *Lanterlu's* from lanterloo or loo, a popular card game. See Epilogue, l. 27.

LUCY

    Yes, madam. (*Aside*) And here I hope we shall find
Master Harcourt.   *Exeunt* ALITHEA, LUCY

Act V, Scene iv

The scene changes again to HORNER'*s lodging*
HORNER, LADY FIDGET, *Mrs* DAINTY FIDGET, *Mrs*
SQUEAMISH. *A table, banquet and bottles*

HORNER (*Aside*)

    A pox! they are come too soon – before I have sent back
my new – mistress. All I have now to do is to lock her
in, that they may not see her.

LADY FIDGET

    That we may be sure of our welcome, we have brought
our entertainment with us, and are resolved to treat   5
thee, dear toad.

DAINTY

    And that we may be merry to purpose, have left Sir
Jaspar and my old Lady Squeamish quarrelling at home
at backgammon.

SQUEAMISH

    Therefore, let us make use of our time, lest they should   10
chance to interrupt us.

LADY FIDGET

    Let us sit then.

HORNER

    First, that you may be private, let me lock this door and
that, and I'll wait upon you presently.

LADY FIDGET

    No, sir, shut 'em only and your lips for ever, for we must   15
trust you as much as our women.

HORNER

    You know all vanity's killed in me; I have no occasion
for talking.

---

2 *new – mistress* He had been going to use some other word.

LADY FIDGET

Now, ladies, supposing we had drank each of us our two
bottles, let us speak the truth of our hearts.   20

DAINTY *and* SQUEAMISH

Agreed.

LADY FIDGET

By this brimmer, for truth is nowhere else to be found.
(*Aside to* HORNER) Not in thy heart, false man!

HORNER (*Aside to* LADY FIDGET)

You have found me a true man, I'm sure!

LADY FIDGET (*Aside to* HORNER)

Not every way. – But let us sit and be merry.   25

LADY FIDGET *sings*

1.

Why should our damned tyrants oblige us to live
On the pittance of pleasure which they only give?
    We must not rejoice
    With wine and with noise.
In vain we must wake in a dull bed alone,   30
Whilst to our warm rival, the bottle, they're gone.
    Then lay aside charms
    And take up these arms.

2.

'Tis wine only gives 'em their courage and wit
Because we live sober, to men we submit.   35
    If for beauties you'd pass
    Take a lick of the glass:
'Twill mend your complexions, and when they are gone
The best red we have is the red of the grape.
    Then, sisters, lay't on,   40
    And damn a good shape.

DAINTY

Dear brimmer! Well, in token of our openness and
plain-dealing, let us throw our masks over our heads.

22 Alluding to the proverb *in vino veritas,* in wine is truth; *brimmer* full glass
25 sd The music for this song is lost.
33 *arms* glasses, as explained by a marginal gloss in Q1–5, O
39 *red* rouge
41 *shape* figure

HORNER

So, 'twill come to the glasses anon.

SQUEAMISH

Lovely brimmer! Let me enjoy him first.   45

LADY FIDGET

No, I never part with a gallant till I've tried him. Dear
brimmer, that mak'st our husbands short-sighted.

DAINTY

And our bashful gallants bold.

SQUEAMISH

And for want of a gallant, the butler lovely in our eyes.
Drink, eunuch.   50

LADY FIDGET

Drink thou representative of a husband. Damn a
husband!

DAINTY

And, as it were a husband, an old keeper.

SQUEAMISH

And an old grandmother.

HORNER

And an English bawd, and a French surgeon.   55

LADY FIDGET

Ay, we have all reason to curse 'em.

HORNER

For my sake, ladies?

LADY FIDGET

No, for our own, for the first spoils all young gallants'
industry.

DAINTY

And the other's art makes 'em bold only with common   60
women.

SQUEAMISH

And rather run the hazard of the vile distemper amongst
them, than of a denial amongst us.

DAINTY

The filthy toads choose mistresses now as they do stuffs,
for having been fancied and worn by others.   65

---

45 *him* This and Lady Fidget's response suggest *brimmer* should be a *double entendre*. Partridge and others record *brim sb.* 'harlot' and *v.* 'to have intercourse'.
55 see I.i. 22–3 and note.
64 *stuffs* cloth

SQUEAMISH

For being common and cheap.

LADY FIDGET

Whilst women of quality, like the richest stuffs, lie untumbled and unasked for.

HORNER

Ay, neat, and cheap, and new, often they think best.

DAINTY

No, sir, the beasts will be known by a mistress longer   70
than by a suit.

SQUEAMISH

And 'tis not for cheapness neither.

LADY FIDGET

No, for the vain fops will take up druggets and embroider 'em. But I wonder at the depraved appetites of witty men; they use to be out of the common road and   75
hate imitation. Pray tell me, beast, when you were a man, why you rather chose to club with a multitude in a common house for an entertainment than to be the only guest at a good table?

HORNER

Why, faith, ceremony and expectation are unsufferable   80
to those that are sharp bent. People always eat with the best stomach at an ordinary, where every man is snatching for the best bit.

LADY FIDGET

Though he get a cut over the fingers. But I have heard people eat most heartily of another man's meat, that is,   85
what they do not pay for.

---

68 *untumbled* (of cloth) unhandled; (of women) unwanted for sex; 'Before you tumbled me, / You promised me to wed' (*Hamlet* IV.v. 62–3)

69 *neat* (of clothes) comparatively plain; (of women) comparatively pure, like Mrs. Pinchwife

73 *druggets* cheap wool fabrics

75 *use to be* are usually

78 *common house* restaurant or perhaps brothel

80 *expectation* waiting

81 *are sharp bent* have a keen appetite

82 *ordinary* restaurant

84 *cut over the fingers* probably alluding to Horner's supposed surgical disaster

HORNER

When they are sure of their welcome and freedom, for ceremony in love and eating is as ridiculous as in fighting. Falling on briskly is all should be done in those occasions.   90

LADY FIDGET

Well then, let me tell you, sir, there is nowhere more freedom than in our houses, and we take freedom from a young person as a sign of good breeding, and a person may be as free as he pleases with us, as frolic, as gamesome, as wild as he will.   95

HORNER

Ha'n't I heard you all declaim against wild men?

LADY FIDGET

Yes, but for all that, we think wildness in a man as desirable a quality as in a duck or rabbit. A tame man, foh!

HORNER

I know not, but your reputations frightened me, as much   100
as your faces invited me.

LADY FIDGET

Our reputation! Lord, why should you not think that we women make use of our reputation, as you men of yours, only to deceive the world with less suspicion? Our virtue is like the statesman's religion, the Quaker's   105
word, the gamester's oath, and the great man's honour – but to cheat those that trust us.

SQUEAMISH

And that demureness, coyness, and modesty that you see in our faces in the boxes at plays is as much a sign of a kind woman as a vizard-mask in the pit.   110

DAINTY

For, I assure you, women are least masked when they have the velvet vizard on.

---

89 *falling on* (in love) having sex, (in eating) starting, (in fighting) attacking
96 *wild* See Etherege's *She Would if she Could* (ed. Charlene M. Taylor) I.ii. 37–9: 'There is
    not such another wild man in the Town. All his talk was of wenching, and swearing, and
    drinking, and tearing'.
98 *desirable* because wild animals yield the best meat (Dixon)
110 *kind* available for sex
    vizard-mask sign of a whore. See I.i. 186 note.

LADY FIDGET
You would have found us modest women in our denials only.

SQUEAMISH
Our bashfulness is only the reflection of the men's.   115

DAINTY
We blush, when they are shamefaced.

HORNER
I beg your pardon, ladies. I was deceived in you devilishly. But why that mighty pretence to honour?

LADY FIDGET
We have told you. But sometimes 'twas for the same reason you men pretend business often, to avoid ill   120
company, to enjoy the better and more privately those you love.

HORNER
But why would you ne'er give a friend a wink then?

LADY FIDGET
Faith, your reputation frightened us as much as ours did you, you were so notoriously lewd.   125

HORNER
And you so seemingly honest.

LADY FIDGET
Was that all that deterred you?

HORNER
And so expensive – you allow freedom, you say? –

LADY FIDGET
Ay, ay.

HORNER
– that I was afraid of losing my little money, as well as   130
my little time, both which my other pleasures required.

LADY FIDGET
Money, foh! You talk like a little fellow now. Do such as we expect money?

HORNER
I beg your pardon, madam. I must confess, I have heard that great ladies, like great merchants, set but the higher   135
prices upon what they have, because they are not in necessity of taking the first offer.

126   *honest* chaste
128   *freedom* plain-dealing

DAINTY

Such as we, make sale of our hearts?

SQUEAMISH

We bribed for our love? Foh!

HORNER

With your pardon, ladies, I know, like great men in 140
offices, you seem to exact flattery and attendance only
from your followers, but you have receivers about you,
and such fees to pay, a man is afraid to pass your grants.
Besides, we must let you win at cards, or we lose your
hearts. And if you make an assignation, 'tis at a 145
goldsmith's, jeweller's, or china house, where, for your
honour you deposit to him, he must pawn his to the
punctual cit, and so paying for what you take up, pays
for what he takes up.

DAINTY

Would you not have us assured of our gallant's love? 150

SQUEAMISH

For love is better known by liberality than by jealousy.

LADY FIDGET

For one may be dissembled, the other not. (*Aside*) But
my jealousy can be no longer dissembled, and they are
telling ripe. – Come, here's to our gallants in waiting,
whom we must name, and I'll begin. This is my false 155
rogue. *Claps him on the back*

SQUEAMISH

How!

HORNER [*Aside*]

So, all will out now.

SQUEAMISH (*Aside to* HORNER)

Did you not tell me, 'twas for my sake only you reported
yourself no man? 160

---

142   *receivers* servants who take bribes
143   *pass your grants* accept your favours
146–8 *for your honour . . . punctual cit* for trusting your honour to him, he must pawn his to
      the punctilious shopkeeper
153–4 *jealousy* Q1–2 4–5, O (jealousies Q3); *they are telling ripe* they (the other ladies) are ready
      to be told. But if Q3 is right, the phrase means they (the jealousies) are ready to be told,
      i.e. very strong.
  154 *gallants in waiting* lovers awaiting our pleasure; phrase coined on the analogy of ladies
      in waiting

DAINTY (*Aside to* HORNER)
Oh wretch! Did you not swear to me, 'twas for my love
and honour you passed for that thing you do?

HORNER
So, so.

LADY FIDGET
Come, speak ladies; this is my false villain.

SQUEAMISH
And mine too.   165

DAINTY
And mine.

HORNER
Well, then, you are all three my false rogues too, and
there's an end on't.

LADY FIDGET
Well, then, there's no remedy; sister sharers, let us not
fall out, but have a care of our honour. Though we get   170
no presents, no jewels of him, we are savers of our
honour, the jewel of most value and use, which shines
yet to the world unsuspected, though it be counterfeit.

HORNER
Nay, and is e'en as good as if it were true, provided the
world think so; for honour, like beauty, now, only   175
depends on the opinion of others.

LADY FIDGET
Well, Harry Common, I hope you can be true to three.
Swear – but 'tis no purpose to require your oath; for
you are as often forsworn as you swear to new women.

HORNER
Come, faith, madam, let us e'en pardon one another, for   180
all the difference I find betwixt we men and you women,
we forswear ourselves at the beginning of an amour, you
as long as it lasts.

Enter SIR JASPAR FIDGET *and* OLD LADY SQUEAMISH

SIR JASPAR
Oh, my Lady Fidget, was this your cunning to come to

---

177 *Harry* Horner's first name; *Common*, i.e. a stud, on the analogy of Doll Common, the
prostitue in *The Alchemist*

Master Horner without me? But you have been nowhere   185
else, I hope.

LADY FIDGET
No, Sir Jaspar.

OLD LADY SQUEAMISH
And you came straight hither, Biddy?

SQUEAMISH
Yes, indeed, lady grandmother.

SIR JASPAR
'Tis well, 'tis well. I knew when once they were   190
thoroughly acquainted with poor Horner they'd ne'er be
from him. You may let her masquerade it with my wife
and Horner, and I warrant her reputation safe.

Enter BOY

BOY
Oh, sir, here's the gentleman come whom you bid me
not suffer to come up without giving you notice, with a   195
lady, too, and other gentlemen.

HORNER
Do you all go in there, whilst I send 'em away, and boy,
do you desire 'em to stay below till I come, which shall
be immediately.
                    Exeunt SIR JASPAR, LADY SQUEAMISH, LADY FIDGET,
                                Mrs DAINTY, SQUEAMISH

BOY
Yes, sir.   *Exit*   200

Exit HORNER *at t'other door, and returns with*
MRS PINCHWIFE

HORNER
You would not take my advice to be gone home before
your husband came back; he'll now discover all. Yet
pray, my dearest, be persuaded to go home, and leave
the rest to my management. I'll let you down the back
way.   205

MRS PINCHWIFE
I don't know the way home, so I don't.

HORNER
My man shall wait upon you.

[180]

MRS PINCHWIFE

No, don't you believe that I'll go at all. What, are you
weary of me already?

HORNER

No, my life, 'tis that I may love you long, 'tis to secure   210
my love, and your reputation with your husband. He'll
never receive you again else.

MRS PINCHWIFE

What care I? D'ye think to frighten me with that? I
don't intend to go to him again. You shall be my
husband now.   215

HORNER

I cannot be your husband, dearest, since you are
married to him.

MRS PINCHWIFE

Oh, would you make me believe that? Don't I see every
day at London here, women leave their first husbands,
and go and live with other men as their wives? Pish,   220
pshaw! You'd make me angry, but that I love you so
mainly.

HORNER

So, they are coming up. – In again, in, I hear 'em.

(*Exit* MRS PINCHWIFE)

Well, a silly mistress is like a weak place, soon got, soon
lost; a man has scarce time for plunder. She betrays her   225
husband first to her gallant, and then her gallant to her
husband.

Enter PINCHWIFE, ALITHEA, HARCOURT, SPARKISH,

LUCY *and a* PARSON

PINCHWIFE

Come, madam, 'tis not the sudden change of your dress,
the confidence of your asseverations, and your false
witness there, shall persuade me I did not bring you   230
hither just now. Here's my witness, who cannot deny it,
since you must be confronted. – Master Horner, did not
I bring this lady to you just now?

222 *mainly* strongly
224 *weak place* ill-defended fortress
230 *witness* i.e., Lucy

[181]

HORNER (*Aside*)

  Now must I wrong one woman for another's sake. But
  that's no new thing with me; for in these cases I am still   235
  on the criminal's side, against the innocent.

ALITHEA

  Pray speak, sir.

HORNER (*Aside*)

  It must be so. I must be impudent and try my luck;
  impudence uses to be too hard for truth.

PINCHWIFE

  What, you are studying an evasion, or excuse for her?   240
  Speak, sir.

HORNER

  No, faith, I am something backward only to speak in
  women's affairs or disputes.

PINCHWIFE

  She bids you speak.

ALITHEA

  Ay, pray sir do, pray satisfy him.   245

HORNER

  Then truly, you did bring that lady to me just now.

PINCHWIFE

  O ho!

ALITHEA

  How, sir!

HARCOURT

  How, Horner!

ALITHEA

  What mean you, sir? I always took you for a man of   250
  honour.

HORNER (*Aside*)

  Ay, so much a man of honour that I must save my
  mistress, I thank you, come what will on't.

SPARKISH

  So, if I had had her, she'd have made me believe the
  moon had been made of a Christmas pie.   255

---

  239 *uses to be* is usually
  254–5 *the moon . . . Christmas pie* i.e., something incredible; usually, that the moon is made of
      green cheese. Perhaps this variant is suggested by Horner's name, as Little Jack Horner
      in the nursery rhyme ate a Christmas pie.

LUCY (*Aside*)

  Now could I speak, if I durst, and solve the riddle, who
  am the author of it.

ALITHEA

  O unfortunate woman! A combination against my honour,
  which most concerns me now, because you share in my
  disgrace, sir, and it is your censure which I must now   260
  suffer that troubles me, not theirs.

HARCOURT

  Madam, then have no trouble, you shall now see 'tis
  possible for me to love too, without being jealous. I will
  not only believe your innocence myself, but make all the
  world believe it. (*Apart to* HORNER) Horner, I must now   265
  be concerned for this lady's honour.

HORNER

  And I must be concerned for a lady's honour too.

HARCOURT

  This lady has her honour, and I will protect it.

HORNER

  My lady has not her honour, but has given it me to keep,
  and I will preserve it.   270

HARCOURT

  I understand you not.

HORNER

  I would not have you.

MRS PINCHWIFE (*Peeping in behind*)

  What's the matter with 'em all?

PINCHWIFE

  Come, come, Master Horner, no more disputing. Here's
  the parson; I brought him not in vain.   275

HARCOURT

  No, sir, I'll employ him, if this lady please.

PINCHWIFE

  How! What d'ye mean?

SPARKISH

  Ay, what does he mean?

---

  256 *solve* Q2–5, O ('solve Q1)
  258 *combination* plot
  276 sp HARCOURT Q5 (*Hor.* Q1–4, O). This speech suits Harcourt rather than Horner, who
     has no intention of marrying Alithea, as his speech at l. 279 shows. An easy printer's
     error.

HORNER

Why, I have resigned your sister to him; he has my
consent.   280

PINCHWIFE

But he has not mine, sir. A woman's injured honour, no
more than a man's can be repaired or satisfied by any
but him that first wronged it. And you shall marry her
presently, or –   *Lays his hand on his sword*

Enter to them MRS PINCHWIFE

MRS PINCHWIFE

O Lord, they'll kill poor Master Horner! Besides he   285
shan't marry her whilst I stand by and look on. I'll not
lose my second husband so.

PINCHWIFE

What do I see?

ALITHEA

My sister in my clothes!

SPARKISH

Ha!   290

MRS PINCHWIFE

Nay, pray now don't quarrel about finding work for the
parson. He shall marry me to Master Horner. (*To*
PINCHWIFE) For now I believe you have enough of me.

HORNER

Damned, damned loving changeling!

MRS PINCHWIFE

Pray, sister, pardon me for telling so many lies of you.   295

HARCOURT

I suppose the riddle is plain now.

LUCY

No, that must be my work. Good sir, hear me.
                          Kneels to PINCHWIFE, *who stands doggedly,*
                                      with his hat over his eyes

PINCHWIFE

I will never hear woman again, but make 'em all silent,
thus –   *Offers to draw upon his wife*

297 sd *doggedly* morosely

HORNER
No, that must not be.   300
PINCHWIFE
You then shall go first, 'tis all one to me.
                    Offers to draw on HORNER; *stopped by* HARCOURT
HARCOURT
Hold!

Enter SIR JASPAR FIDGET, LADY FIDGET, LADY SQUEAMISH,
          Mrs DAINTY FIDGET, *Mrs* SQUEAMISH

SIR JASPAR
What's the matter? what's the matter? pray, what's the
matter, sir? I beseech you communicate, sir.
PINCHWIFE
Why, my wife has communicated, sir, as your wife may   305
have done too, sir, if she knows him, sir.
SIR JASPAR
Pshaw! with him! ha, ha, he!
PINCHWIFE
D'ye mock me, sir? A cuckold is a kind of a wild beast,
have a care, sir!
SIR JASPAR
No, sure, you mock me, sir. He cuckold you! It can't   310
be, ha, ha, he! Why, I'll tell you, sir –   *Offers to whisper*
PINCHWIFE
I tell you again, he has whored my wife, and yours too, if
he knows her, and all the women he comes near. 'Tis
not his dissembling, his hypocrisy, can wheedle me.
SIR JASPAR
How! does he dissemble? Is he a hypocrite? Nay, then –   315
how – wife – sister, is he an hypocrite?
OLD LADY SQUEAMISH
An hypocrite, a dissembler! Speak, young harlotry,
speak, how?
SIR JASPAR
Nay, then – Oh, my head too! – Oh thou libidinous lady!

---

305 *communicated* had sexual intercourse
308 Possibly Pinchwife threatens to draw his sword again here, and at ll. 347 and 364.
319 *my head* i.e., he begins to feel he is a cuckold

OLD LADY SQUEAMISH
Oh thou harloting harlotry! Hast thou done't then?   320

SIR JASPAR
Speak, good Horner, art thou a dissembler, a rogue?
Hast thou –

HORNER
Soh –

LUCY (*Apart to* HORNER)
I'll fetch you off, and her too, if she will but hold her
tongue.   325

HORNER (*Apart to* LUCY)
Canst thou? I'll give thee –

LUCY (*To* PINCHWIFE)
Pray, have but patience to hear me, sir, who am the
unfortunate cause of all this confusion. Your wife is
innocent, I only culpable; for I put her upon telling you
all these lies concerning my mistress in order to the   330
breaking off the match between Master Sparkish and
her, to make way for Master Harcourt.

SPARKISH
Did you so, eternal rotten-tooth? Then it seems my
mistress was not false to me, I was only deceived by you.
Brother that should have been, now man of conduct,   335
who is a frank person now – to bring your wife to her
lover – ha?

LUCY
I assure you, sir, she came not to Master Horner out of
love, for she loves him no more –

MRS PINCHWIFE
Hold, I told lies for you, but you shall tell none for me,   340
for I do love Master Horner with all my soul, and
nobody shall say me nay. Pray don't you go to make
poor Master Horner believe to the contrary; 'tis
spitefully done of you, I'm sure.

HORNER (*Aside to* MRS PINCHWIFE)
Peace, dear idiot!   345

323 *soh* Possibly Horner sighs, like Mrs Pinchwife at IV.ii. 130, though there Q1–5, O have a
stage-direction.
324 *she* i.e., Mrs Pinchwife, who soon interrupts Lucy as we expect
335 *man of conduct* you who tell us how to conduct ourselves
336 *frank* i.e., Pinchwife's sarcasm (III.ii. 360) is thrown back at him

MRS PINCHWIFE
  Nay, I will not peace.

PINCHWIFE
  Not till I make you.

Enter DORILANT, QUACK

DORILANT
  Horner, your servant; I am the doctor's guest, he must
  excuse our intrusion.

QUACK
  But what's the matter, gentlemen? For heaven's sake,   350
  what's the matter?

HORNER
  Oh, 'tis well you are come. 'Tis a censorious world we
  live in; you may have brought me a reprieve, or else I
  had died for a crime I never committed, and these
  innocent ladies had suffered with me. Therefore, pray   355
  satisfy these worthy, honourable, jealous gentlemen –
  that –   *Whispers*

QUACK
  Oh, I understand you; is that all? –   Sir Jaspar, by
  heavens and upon the word of a physician sir –
                                        Whispers to SIR JASPAR

SIR JASPAR
  Nay, I do believe you truly. – Pardon me, my virtuous   360
  lady, and dear of honour.

OLD LADY SQUEAMISH
  What, then all's right again?

SIR JASPAR
  Ay, ay, and now let us satisfy him too.
                                  They whisper with PINCHWIFE

PINCHWIFE
  An eunuch! Pray, no fooling with me.

QUACK
  I'll bring half the surgeons in town to swear it.   365

---

352 *censorious world* This echoes Lady Fidget's phrase at IV.iii. 62
354 *had* should have
361 *dear of honour* See II.i. 412 note.

PINCHWIFE

They! – They'll swear a man that bled to death through his wounds died of an apoplexy.

QUACK

Pray hear me, sir. Why, all the town has heard the report of him.

PINCHWIFE

But does all the town believe it?   370

QUACK

Pray enquire a little, and first of all these.

PINCHWIFE

I'm sure when I left the town he was the lewdest fellow in't.

QUACK

I tell you, sir, he has been in France since; pray ask but these ladies and gentlemen, your friend Master   375
Dorilant. – Gentlemen and ladies, ha'n't you all heard the late sad report of poor Master Horner?

ALL LADIES

Ay, ay, ay.

DORILANT

Why, thou jealous fool, do'st thou doubt it? He's an arrant French capon.   380

MRS PINCHWIFE

'Tis false, sir, you shall not disparage poor Master Horner, for to my certain knowledge –

LUCY

Oh hold!

SQUEAMISH (*Aside to* LUCY)

Stop her mouth!

LADY FIDGET (*To* PINCHWIFE)

Upon my honour, sir, 'tis as true –   385

DAINTY

D'ye think we would have been seen in his company?

SQUEAMISH

Trust our unspotted reputations with him!

366–7 Doctors sometimes perjured themselves about the causes of deaths through duelling, as it was illegal.

  380 *capon* castrated cock, eunuch

385, 388   sp LADY FIDGET cd. (*Old. La. Fid.* Q1–5, O).

LADY FIDGET (*Aside to* HORNER)

This you get, and we too, by trusting your secret to a
fool.

HORNER

Peace, madam. (*Aside to* QUACK) Well, doctor, is not   390
this a good design, that carries a man on unsuspected,
and brings him off safe?

PINCHWIFE (*Aside*)

Well, if this were true; but my wife –

                    DORILANT *whispers with* MRS PINCHWIFE

ALITHEA

Come, brother, your wife is yet innocent you see. But
have a care of too strong an imagination, lest like an   395
over-concerned, timorous gamester, by fancying an
unlucky cast, it should come. Women and fortune are
truest still to those that trust 'em.

LUCY

And any wild thing grows but the more fierce and
hungry for being kept up, and more dangerous to the   400
keeper.

ALITHEA

There's doctrine for all husbands, Master Harcourt.

HARCOURT

I edify, madam, so much that I am impatient till I am
one.

DORILANT

And I edify so much by example I will never be one.   405

SPARKISH

And because I will not disparage my parts I'll ne'er be
one.

HORNER

And I, alas, can't be one.

393 sd What do they whisper about? She perhaps tells him Horner is not impotent, and he
     perhaps tells her she can't marry Horner and must deceive Pinchwife.
403 *edify* profit spiritually from Alithea's 'doctrine'; a Puritan term, used with mock solemnity
406 sp SPARKISH Q2–5, O (*Eew.* Q1). The Q1 reading baffles all editors.
     disparage my pans lower myself (by an unequal match); echoing what he said at II.i. 289
     but with a different meaning

PINCHWIFE

But I must be one – against my will, to a country wife,
with a country murrain to me.   410

MRS PINCHWIFE (*Aside*)

And I must be a country wife still too, I find, for I can't,
like a city one, be rid of my musty husband and do what
I list.

HORNER

Now, sir, I must pronounce your wife innocent, though I
blush whilst I do it, and I am the only man by her now   415
exposed to shame, which I will straight drown in wine,
as you shall your suspicion, and the ladies' troubles we'll
divert with a ballet. Doctor, where are your maskers?

LUCY

Indeed, she's innocent, sir, I am her witness. And her
end of coming out was but to see her sister's wedding,   420
and what she has said to your face of her love to Master
Horner was but the usual innocent revenge on a
husband's jealousy – was it not, madam? Speak.

MRS PINCHWIFE (*Aside to* LUCY *and* HORNER)

Since you'll have me tell more lies. – Yes, indeed, bud.

PINCHWIFE

For my own sake fain I would all believe;   425
Cuckolds like lovers should themselves deceive.
But – (*Sighs*) –
His honour is least safe, too late I find,
Who trusts it with a foolish wife or friend.

---

410   *murrain* cattle plague; 'he talks as like a grazier as he looks', as mentioned at I.i. 343
418   *ballet* dance in masquerade
      Doctor, where are your maskers? Holger M. Klein suggests the question should be put to
      Sir Jaspar, who promised 'fiddles' (V.ii.102), perhaps implying masqueraders (*Archiv*, vol.
      211 (1974), 66–8). But Sir Jaspar would not have provided a *dance of cuckolds* (l. 429);
      Quack probably would, and he and Horner seem to be plotting something at V.ii.110–11.
      Such final dances were conventional in comedy and needed little explanation.
420   *end of* purpose in
429   sd The final dance does not express the harmony of conventional comedy. Weales argues
      that if it is to have the effect of poking fun at Pinchwife and Sir Jaspar it must be set to
      music associated with cuckolds, and suggests the tune 'Cuckolds in a Row', which was
      readily available in John Playford's *The Dancing Master*. But as Weales says, Pepys saw
      Charles II dancing to this tune in December 1662; surely the comic effect could have been
      achieved more reliably by having the masqueraders wear horns.

A dance of cuckolds

HORNER

    Vain fops, but court, and dress, and keep a pother   430
    To pass for women's men with one another;
    But he who aims by women to be prized,
    First by the men, you see, must be despised.   [*Exeunt*]

430 *keep a pother* make a fuss
433 sd ed. Q1 does not have an *exeunt* here; it has '*FINIS*' lower down the page, and 'FINIS'
    again after the epilogue on the next page. Many but not all late seventeenth-century play
    quartos have an *exeunt* or *exeunt omnes* after the last line of the play and before the epi-
    logue; but the stage business is not obvious. At the end of *The Man of Mode* (1676) Old
    Bellair says 'So now we'll in' and addresses '*to the pit*' a couplet requesting applause; this
    is followed by an *exeunt omnes* and an epilogue. In Restoration productions generally
    the curtain was probably not lowered till after the epilogue (Pierre Danchin, privately).
    So I suggest that in a modern production of *The Country Wife* the players should all go
    off after Horner's final speech, and come back for the applause; then the actress playing
    Lady Fidget should step forward as herself, and speak the epilogue.

EPILOGUE

Spoken by Mrs Knepp

Now, you the vigorous, who daily here
O'er vizard-mask in public domineer,
And what you'd do to her if in place where;
Nay, have the confidence to cry 'Come out!'
Yet when she says 'Lead on' you are not stout;   5
But to your well-dressed brother straight turn round
And cry 'Pox on her, Ned, she can't be sound!'
Then slink away, a fresh one to engage,
With so much seeming heat and loving rage,
You'd frighten listening actress on the stage;   10
Till she at last has seen you huffing come
And talk of keeping in the tiring-room,
Yet cannot be provoked to lead her home.
Next, you Falstaff s of fifty, who beset
Your buckram maidenheads, which your friends get;   15
And whilst to them you of achievements boast,
They share the booty, and laugh at your cost.
In fine, you essenced boys, both old and young,
Who would be thought so eager, brisk, and strong,
Yet do the ladies, not their husbands, wrong;   20
Whose purses for your manhood make excuse,

Mrs Knepp Q2–5, O (Mr *Hart* Q1). Obviously the epilogue should be spoken by an actress.
2 *vizard-mask* See I.i. 186 note.
3 *if in place where* if you were in a convenient place
4 *'Come out!'* Come out and fight
5 stout brave
7 *sound* See V.ii. 47 note.
11 *huffing* See Prologue, l. 19 note.
12 *keeping* See I.i. 405–6 note
   tiring-room See Prologue, l. 25 note.
14–17 These lines refer to *Henry IV, Part I* II.iv, where Falstaff boasts of having fought numerous 'rogues in buckram suits' after the Gadshill robbery, though he has in fact run away. His friends Prince Hal and Poins have shared the booty and have the last laugh. Similarly elderly gallants boast of their conquests to the young men who have actually had the women.
18 *essenced* perfumed

And keep your Flanders mares for show, not use;
Encouraged by our woman's man today,
A Horner's part may vainly think to play;
And may intrigues so bashfully disown   25
That they may doubted be by few or none;
May kiss the cards at picquet, ombre, loo,
And so be thought to kiss the lady too;
But, gallants, have a care, faith, what you do.
The world, which to no man his due will give,   30
You by experience know you can deceive,
And men may still believe you vigorous,
But then we women – there's no coz'ning us!

FINIS

22 *Flanders mares* (literally) horses for the heavy coaches of the aristocracy, a status symbol; (metaphorically) kept women or prostitutes
24–6 i.e., the boys may pretend embarrassment in the hope of getting a false reputation for being rakes
27 *kiss the cards* i.e., make a flirtatious gesture
    piquet, ombre, loo fashionable card games
33 *coz'ning* cozening, deceiving

NOTES

NOTES

NOTES

NOTES

NOTES

NOTES

NOTES

NOTES

NOTES